FIVE HABITS
OF
HIGH-IMPACT
MANAGERS

FIVE HABITS
OF
HIGH-IMPACT
MANAGERS

ALLEN E. FISHMAN

Five Habits of High-Impact Managers

Published by Direct Communication Service, Inc.

Copyright © 2016 by Allen E. Fishman

Direct Communication Service, Inc

11031 Sheridan Blvd.

Westminster, Colorado USA 800250

Printed in the United States of America.

2016 – First Edition

Book cover design: 99designs.com

Interior layout and design by: AuthorSupport.com

For further information about AlignUp training – please visit www.AlignUptraining.com

This book was possible only as a result of
the outstanding contributions made by members of
the TAB community throughout the world.

CONTENTS

INTRODUCTION

The principles of the High Impact Manager program were first developed when I was co-owner and president of a company that was so successful that we were able to take it public on the stock exchange. Then, in 1990, I formed a company, TAB Boards International, Inc. (TAB), which is currently the world's largest peer advisory group and coaching franchise system.

Shortly after forming TAB, it was obvious to me that most organizations that joined TAB had not been achieving their greatest potential for success. Their executives and other managers were simply not bringing about the highest impact that they were capable of providing. Over a period of time, I identified 24 habits that were typically shared by high impact managers (High Impact Managers) to move their organizations to a higher level of success.

I've tried to turn each of these habits into real world knowledge, which can be applied to help executive and managers. This book focuses on 5 habits that will help you to become a High Impact Manager.

I formed Allen Training Centers, Inc. (ATC) to provide executives and other managers with the practical knowledge they need to become High Impact Managers who make lasting, positive change within their organizations and their own lives. ATC (www.allentrainingcenters.com) provides training programs, including the High Impact Manager training program that involves 24 in-person sessions with two different habits focused on in each training session. Those managers who take the training also receive online learning that covers each of the 24 topics. For those managers unable to attend live High Impact Manager training, they can take the online training at their own pace.

I decided to write this book after recognizing the challenge organizations throughout the world face—because their managers aren't able to engineer the greatest impact for their companies.

Many factors separate High-Impact Managers from other managers. High-Impact Managers understand how to negotiate more effectively. They manage their time more effectively. They recruit and hire more effectively and they also display certain habits that make them more effective.

In this book, my approach is to first identify those habits High-Impact Managers around the world have in common. I then explore these habits in easy-to-follow, point-by-point ways that any manager can use to bring about greater impact on his or her organization.

HABIT 1

Setting New Employees Up For Success

Managers often do all the right things in recruiting, selecting and hiring new employees. Immediately thereafter, they treat them as if they have been working for the company for a long time. There's no structure for onboarding and integrating new employees during an orientation period, which is critically important for making the new employee feel like he or she belongs and understand how he or she fits in.

Without a plan for integration, your new employees will be less effective at their jobs. They won't have the institutional knowledge needed to help them do their jobs better and it will take longer for them to feel like they are part of the organization. As a result, they will be more susceptible to the many factors that could result in them leaving the company before giving the new job a real chance.

In contrast, High-Impact Managers employ a New Employee Orientation Checklist, starting on day one of employment. Using a clear formal checklist, they aim to get new employees quickly thinking of themselves as part of the organization's community. This makes them more likely to become valuable long-term employees.

High-Impact Managers do what is needed to encourage employees to become more engaged with and dedicated to the organization. They create an environment that instills passion and commitment, where employees genuinely enjoy being part of the organization's community.

> **Use the orientation period as a "re-recruitment opportunity."**

Here are 20 of the most common checklist items High-Impact Managers use for setting up their new employees for success, starting on the first day of employment.

- Item #1: New Employee's First Day of Work
- Item #2: Provide Clarity about Expectations
- Item #3: Review Employee Job Descriptions
- Item #4: Review Your Functional Organization Chart
- Item #5: Communicate Work Hours Expectations
- Item #6: Assign Mentor
- Item #7: Long-term Employees Share Meal with New Employee
- Item #8: Train Current Employees on how to Help with Onboarding New Employee
- Item #9: Introductions of New Employee by Boss
- Item #10: Share Knowledge about Your Organization's Products and Services
- Item #11: Review Personnel Handbook
- Item #12: Share Long-term Organization Vision, Mission and Culture
- Item #13: Review Written Protocols, Processes and Procedures

- Item #14: Organization's Personal Internet, Phone and Texting Policies
- Item #15: Communicate Professional Dress Code Policies
- Item #16: Communicate Sexual Harassment Policy
- Item #17: Communicate Policy about Second Jobs
- Item #18: Communicate Policy About Regularly Scheduled Reviews
- Item #19: Communicate Unexcused Absence Policy
- Item #20: Discuss Department/Team Goals, Objectives, and Measurements

ITEM #1: NEW EMPLOYEE'S FIRST DAY OF WORK

How many times have you seen a new employee, regardless of position, stuck in a corner of the office because things weren't ready for his or her first day? This unfavorable first impression will remain with employees in a way that colors their desire to stay with the company (even if it doesn't rear its ugly head for a few years.)

Just as we all form a first impression of people we meet, it's important that your new employees have a great first impression of what it's like to work for your organization. Be prepared to make that great first impression.

What day of the week is best to start new employees? Many High-Impact Managers won't start new employees on a Monday or Friday. On Monday, other employees are busy catching up on work after the weekend and are less likely to offer needed attention to a new employee. Fridays aren't advised because the last day of the workweek isn't enough time to settle in with orientation needs.

ITEM #2: PROVIDE CLARITY ABOUT EXPECTATIONS

Employees who have clarity on job performance expectations are less likely to become frustrated at work. One reason good employees look for a new job is that they didn't understand what was expected of them or whether they were progressing towards these undefined expectations.

It's not enough to set specific goals and due dates without following up with discussions on how things are proceeding. Schedule one-on-one reviews with your subordinates—once a week, rather than monthly or only at the end of the year. (For purposes of this program, I will refer to these regularly scheduled meetings as "weekly meetings.")

Give evaluation feedback to your employees on their performances. They need to hear during their one-on-one weekly reviews whether or not they are doing their jobs right and if they are progressing in the right direction. Share favorable feedback regarding areas of top-level job performance. Let them know you're aware that results are being achieved. Acknowledge whenever you see progress.

In the increasingly hectic pace in which most organizations function today, a single conversation at the end of the year is pointless. Instead, High-Impact Managers conduct mini-performance reviews during each of their regularly scheduled meetings with employees.

Before you can discuss performance evaluations, of course, you need to identify three or four key accomplishments that each employee must attain within the next year of employment. If these accomplishments aren't spelled out clearly, employees will start to question their value to the organization; this questioning can lead to a search for new employment.

Meet regularly to discuss evaluations with each of your direct reports. Discuss, among other things, the priorities of what they are to be doing and how things are progressing. Discuss setbacks, if any.

Your responsibility also includes offering clear performance expectations, such as:

- "Develop a global marketing plan within the first six months that will increase profit margins by at least 15%."
- "Work with customers, engineering and operations to identify two new products that can be launched by the end of next year. These products must produce a margin of X."
- "Identify within the first nine months at least two new potential markets for our products with the potential to generate at least X dollars of revenue within one year."
- "Oversee the successful launch of product X, scheduled for the second quarter of next year. Ensure that the launch takes place on time and within budget.

Next, design a form for tracking results. Many downloadable apps will help you design a form that serves your purpose.

During your weekly meetings, the more measurable data you use, the better. Again, apps can help track these key performance indicator measurements. An enormous amount of information can be tracked on a real-time basis through the use of these apps and other resources.

ITEM #3: REVIEW EMPLOYEE JOB DESCRIPTIONS

The more questions employees have about their job responsibilities, the more likely it is you won't retain them. One way to reduce these unknowns is by creating clear employee job descriptions. Employees need to know what actions they can take on their own and what should be cleared with you first. Buying decisions, for example. What decisions can they make without getting your OK beforehand (while also needing to keep you informed)? What actions should they take only *after* obtaining your go-ahead? Make clear these are decisions for which you retain veto power.

> When an employee's work assignments don't match his or her written job description, it is likely to result in employee frustration.

Job descriptions should specify to whom the employee reports, as well as how performance will be measured. If possible, include a "Standards and Measurements of Performance" as part of the employee's evaluation form. Without this element, the performance review system will lack proper communication and "closure." This is critical to making the process a true performance review.

Periodically, rewrite job descriptions so they reflect changes in responsibility. The first time you do this should take place after about six months of employment. You and the new employee should have an opportunity to rewrite the position description.

ITEM #4: REVIEW YOUR FUNCTIONAL ORGANIZATION CHART

Another way to reduce unknowns is by creating a "functional organization chart" that lists all of the primary functions assigned to positions in your organization. This chart represents more than just a reporting relationship chart with lines and boxes. It should include:

- Effective date of the chart
- Title for each position
- Basic function (one to two sentences expressed in broad terms such as, "the basic function of the Chief Operating Officer is to plan, organize, direct, coordinate and control the organization in such a way as to meet the growth, profit and cultural objectives of the organization as determined by its CEO and board of directors.")
- Reporting relationships (both up and down)
- Authority (defined)
- Responsibilities (defined)
- Principle duties
- Standards and measurements of performance

> **Even though the new employee's job description was, hopefully, discussed with the new employee at the time of hiring, go through this job description again.**

ITEM #5: COMMUNICATE WORK-HOUR EXPECTATIONS

You can reduce the likelihood of talented subordinates leaving due to feeling overworked if you communicate work-hour expectations with them. Also, explain that there will be times when more work is needed. For example, you may want the individual to understand that during some weeks, he or she will be expected to work whatever hours are necessary because of urgent problems that must be addressed. If this expectation is left unexplained, it will result in situations where your subordinates are resentful at having to put in long hours and feel you are taking advantage and overworking them.

Ask yourself whether it is necessary for salaried employees to work as many evenings and weekends as you presently request. If the answer is no, then let them know these are not expectations you have for them. This will reduce the chances of them seeking another position where they won't have to work excessive hours.

Also, review your Paid Time Off (PTO) policy. Does it create an incentive to stay with the organization? Are there additional benefits based upon longevity of employment? What about a policy that gives your employees time off *in addition* to holidays, sick time, vacation time and other days mandated by your country, state or province? Many organizations, large and small, offer additional PTO (with the number of days starting at a smaller rate for the first year of employment and increasing up to a maximum number of days after 10 years). Some organizations bundle personal time off with sick days and some bundle them with vacation days.

What about "floating holidays"? Consider a policy in which an employee who has been with your organization a long time is entitled to an increased number of floating holidays, which he or she can use at a time of their choosing. These floating holidays can be one, two or three days (or as many as you want to offer) and used all at once or separately. If allowed by the laws under which you operate, specify that these floating holidays can be used for religious holidays for those who desire to observe them. (This way, you don't need to give time off for holidays for each religion.)

Do you have a policy concerning unpaid leave? Many organizations retain employees by granting them leave without pay to cope with personal situations.

ITEM #6: ASSIGN A MENTOR

A mentor should be assigned to each new employee. Doing so will generate feelings of acceptance that propel that employee to become productive much faster.

For hourly employees, this can take place within the first thirty to ninety days of employment. For managerial-level employees, the period is typically much longer and may last throughout the first year of employment.

Consider offering a monetary bonus to the designated mentor at the end of the mentoring period (if the new employee remains with the organization). Mentors should also be informed of what is expected of them in this role.

ITEM #7: LONG-TERM EMPLOYEES SHARE MEAL WITH NEW EMPLOYEE

Some long-term employees will go out of their way to make a new employee feel welcome; unfortunately, if expectations are not clear, other long-timers will not.

Ask a long-term employee (or more than one) to "break bread" with your new employee. Assign different, well-respected longer-term employees to invite the new employee to lunch (paid for by the organization) during the first week of work. So, you will need to train your current employees to make the mealtime a great experience. The veteran employee must understand his or her obligation to make the new employee feel at home. For example, the hosting employee can ask the new employee questions that are not work-related, such as family-focused topics, which help accelerate the bonding process.

Here are some of the many benefits that come from shared meals:

- Long-term employees promote your organization as a great place to work.
- The new employee feels that longer-term employees expect them to succeed.
- Long-term employees share their wealth of knowledge about the organization.

ITEM #8: TRAIN CURRENT EMPLOYEES ON HOW TO HELP WITH ONBOARDING NEW EMPLOYEE

Make it clear what you expect from your current workforce during the new employee's onboarding period. Set up a training session for these employees to illustrate how important it is to make the right impression on new employees. Training may also include what is expected of them in interacting with a new employee.

> Watch out for long-term employees who resent new employees and might make negative feelings known to them.

Train your direct reports on positive interpersonal communications and relationship-building techniques. These include employing good eye contact, a friendly handshake and willingness to give instructions, as well as a proper introduction to other employees, active listening, feedback, and patience.

ITEM #9: INTRODUCTIONS OF NEW EMPLOYEE BY THE BOSS

The person to whom new employees report should personally take them around and introduce them to those employees with whom they are likely to interact. (You do not need to do these introductions as part of the hiring process.)

If a new employee is at a managerial level, hold an organization-wide staff meeting on the first day of work, during which you can introduce him or her to employees. This is an excellent way to make the new manager feel welcome and a part of the team.

ITEM #10: SHARE KNOWLEDGE ABOUT YOUR ORGANIZATION'S PRODUCTS AND SERVICES

All new employees, regardless of position, need some degree of knowledge about the organization's products or services. But don't overwhelm them information at the same deep level required by sales staff or marketing people. The best approach is to provide a formal presentation on your organization's history and its products and services. Don't assume that your new employee understands these in depth, even if they were explained as part of the hiring process. Also, leave time for questions and answers after the presentation. Often a Human Resources person does this formal presentation. Marketing materials and short videos should be used as well.

Make sure new employees have an opportunity to "test drive" the products or services themselves. The best way to understand something is to see and/or use it in action.

ITEM #11: REVIEW THE PERSONNEL HANDBOOK

With your new employee, review each section of your organization's personnel handbook. Your employee handbook should have a clearly written basis for actions such as discipline, discharge, transfer or changes in job duties. Many handbooks also include such things as the method for evaluations, pay and performance policy, benefit programs, pension and profit sharing plans.

> **Because of the laws in some areas, your attorneys may recommend against published handbooks.**

Having a set of written work rules and clear penalties for violations will help remove some of the fear of the unknown for employees. Organizations without written policies and practices, whether in a handbook form or not, are vulnerable to a new employee's misunderstanding.

This is a good opportunity to check that the practices and policies in your handbook are accurate and up-to-date. Be sure to remove any language that conflicts with current regulatory laws.

Having a published handbook (print or virtual) improves employee morale, prevents disagreements and helps to keep your organization out of court. As a rule, your handbook should not strive to be all-encompassing—shorter is almost always better. Of course, the handbook is of limited value if employees don't read and understand it. As noted, keep the handbook updated on a regular basis, in order to comply with the constantly changing environment of human resources policies.

Depending upon the laws in your area, your attorneys may recommend that in order to protect your organization from potential liability, it is best to get your new employee to sign an acknowledgment that he or she has read and reviewed the personnel policy with someone from your organization. In such cases, there are no excuses for the employee not knowing your organization policies.

ITEM #12: SHARE LONG-TERM ORGANIZATION VISION, MISSION AND CULTURE

People like to feel that what they do is connected to the organization's success and culture. A formal presentation with each new employee is the best time to share the long-term vision for your organization, as well as your mission statement and culture statement, if you have them.

Knowing the vision, mission and culture will give the new employee a feeling of being part of something bigger than him or herself, a feeling of being part of something beyond the work team that he or she works with each day. In a broader sense, it is about being with an organization that will be here long into the future.

Your employee handbook should spell out ramifications that will be followed if policies are violated, such as an oral reprimand, written reprimand, final warning and termination.

Set aside time during the first week in your new employee's job to discuss the long-term vision. Start by asking your new employee to silently read, in front of you, your organization's written vision statement. Although this statement will be clear to you, it may not be clearly understood by someone who has never worked for your organization. So, ask questions to determine if your employee understands the vision.

Every organization should have a vision statement. But if you don't have such a statement in writing, share with the new employee your thoughts about what the organization's long-term vision is.

ITEM #13: REVIEW WRITTEN PROTOCOLS, PROCESSES AND PROCEDURES

Organizations with a great workplace environment have clarity on what needs to be done by each employee. This includes protocols, processes and procedures, hopefully in writing, that you expect your new employee to follow. They must be shared with the new employee. Take time to explain these protocols, processes, and procedures in a way that is as clear and as easy as possible to understand.

ITEM #14: COMMUNICATE ORGANIZATION'S PERSONAL INTERNET, PHONE AND TEXTING POLICY

When your organization has rules in place for the personal use of internet, phone and texting and you don't properly inform new employees, you are asking for problems.

What is your position about employees' non-business use of the internet at work? Many managers feel that to insure productivity, no inappropriate or unsafe computer use should be allowed. This policy addresses computer and e-mail usage, internet usage, workplace monitoring, security inspections and social networking.

Another approach is to wait until someone misuses the web or personal email, before making this a stumbling block.

If your business has restrictive personal technology use policies, your Information Systems expert should partner with you in enforcing the policies (including how long an employee spends on the internet, as well as the sites visited). Random checks can be conducted or computers can be investigated when someone is suspected of poor productivity due to excessive internet usage. Generally, more mild offenses receive a reprimand or warning for the first offense. The reality is that all people will use the internet for personal use to some small degree (possibly during lunch), but true offenders will abuse the privilege for hours per day, practically every day.

Clearly state the need for the policy, and make it clear, with specific language such as, "The organization server may not be used for personal messages or sending jokes of any type. Failure to comply is grounds for immediate dismissal without notice."

Many employees seem to think that personal communications on organization time doesn't count if it is on their own smart phones. As a result, some organizations require that cellular phones be turned off during working hours.

ITEM #15: COMMUNICATE PROFESSIONAL DRESS CODE POLICIES

If you have a clearly articulated dress code, communicate this on the first day to your new employee. First, check with your attorney on what can be put in the dress code and how your organization should handle infractions. Usually these types of codes result from a high-level meeting to discuss appropriate dress code for all employees.

If your code requires all employees to keep appropriate body parts covered, it may or may not be a problem with some new employees, particularly younger employees. The best course of action in these circumstances is for you to have a one-on-one with the employee and to make clear that the dress code has been created so no one's attire becomes a distraction in the workplace.

Since business attire is not equivalent to social attire, normally stating that people should dress "professionally" should be enough, even though it is a bit ambiguous. Ultimately, however, even lengthy dress codes should be written to acknowledge that management may, from time to time, point out specific out-of-bound selections.

It is common to institute a "uniform" requirement for some types of positions, such as a shirt that is appropriately sized, or a mandate that everyone wears the same uniform. The expense of a uniform will have the added benefit of creating a sense of "team," providing visible name recognition when the employees are dressed and out in the public shopping, buying gas, etc.

ITEM #16: COMMUNICATE SEXUAL HARASSMENT POLICY

Inquire about the sexual harassment laws that relate to your organization and have a professional create a detailed discipline policy that includes employee education/training on this subject. The policy should define disciplinary actions in accordance with the frequency and type of harassment.

ITEM #17: COMMUNICATE POLICY ABOUT SECOND JOBS

Clearly establish it if you allow employees to have second jobs. Some organizations permit it, so long as there is no conflict of interest, such as with a competitor. Many High-Impact Managers will not allow a second job because of concerns it will impact job performance, like falling asleep, not finishing projects, etc. Note, in some areas you cannot legally make a policy about an employee's time outside of work.

ITEM #18: COMMUNICATE POLICY ABOUT REGULARLY SCHEDULED REVIEWS

There is usually a "honeymoon period" when you hire a new employee. Sometimes he or she is eager to learn and do whatever is needed for a few weeks, and not so much after that.

It is important to monitor performance closely for the first few weeks, and realize that, after the employee "settles in," there will be a change. Reserve your true evaluation for after the honeymoon period, three months after he or she has come onboard.

Giving praise in a job review to an employee who doesn't deserve it often comes back to haunt the employer who later wants to fire that employee for poor performance. Disciplinary actions are made more difficult by inflated performance reviews. (One example involved the proposed termination of an engineer for "poor performance" whose file had reviews noting "good" for the past three years.)

Commitment to regularly scheduled employee evaluations shows good faith and fair dealings on the employer's part. Evaluations of personnel should be scheduled at intervals of not more than one year. This reduces the risk of an employee not knowing where he or she stands within the organization.

It's important that the new employee understand that this evaluation will be fair, truthful, specific and not overly laudatory. Explain what facts will be collected to review and evaluate the new employee according to their job description. Commit to being open-minded enough to listen to what the employee has to say about the evaluation.

Explain to your new employee that the performance review process begins from the moment the job description is created and agreed to by all parties involved. Set a goal for each primary responsibility so that the evaluation becomes a review of *performance* to the goals.

Create an objective review that is as measurable as possible about expectations for results to be achieved. Prioritizing of performance criteria must be very clear so as to avoid any confusion.

Creating the actual form is easy, once you have established the process. The form you use needs to be no more than a statement of the goal and the performance against that goal. For example, a job description might include "To increase billings by bringing in new customers as measured in dollars billed from new customers." If you lack any measurable standard, it is difficult to come to an objective conclusion on the quality of performance.

ITEM #19: COMMUNICATE UNEXCUSED ABSENCE POLICY

New hires should always be informed about your policy on unexcused/unexplained absences. Typically, such policies provide that an employee absent for some period of time (such as three consecutive days, without prior notice) will be deemed to have voluntarily resigned. This may happen if an employee experiences a death in the family or some other cataclysm resulting in a prolonged (and unexplained) absence. If you reach a point where you need to fill a position with someone else, the last thing you need is concern over a wrongful termination claim if/when the prodigal employee returns to the fold.

ITEM #20: DISCUSS DEPARTMENT/TEAM GOALS, OBJECTIVES, AND MEASUREMENTS

In most workplace environments, some tasks are performed in a team or department structure. Develop an atmosphere that fosters commitment to your organization mission, to your supervisors, and to your team of employees. Show them "what's in it for them." One way to do this is by creating a department or team mission statement and making it come to life.

CONCLUSION

Being effective in bringing on new employees makes their impact much greater and sooner on your organization. Review all 20 of the checklist items. Write down those you should incorporate into your organization to set up your new employees for success.

HABIT 2

Inspiring Leadership

High Impact Managers create superb organization results because they demonstrate an unwavering resolve to do what must be done, as well as set the standard for building a great, enduring organization. High Impact Managers have different leadership styles, but certain basic skill sets must be applied to become an Inspirational Leader.

To inspire your subordinates, you need to have their trust and their respect. Inspirational Leaders help their employees motivate themselves to higher levels of performance. They help employees create a positive work atmosphere in which they are likely to *act* positively.

Inspirational Leaders have a resilient mindset focusing on what needs to be done to succeed. Their attitude includes an unshakeable belief that you are capable of finding the solution. Employees feed off this

> **"When you were made a leader, you weren't given a crown; you were given the responsibility to bring out the best in others." – Jack Welch in "Winning"**

> "In life, you're going to get knocked down sometimes. No one is successful all the time. Learn to brush off your bottom, spit in your palms and say, 'I think I'll go another round.' Then you'll be a winner."
> – George Foreman, at 45, the oldest heavyweight boxing champion

type of unshakeable belief that they can make their organization succeed. To do this, Inspirational Leaders must believe in themselves. If they don't, employees won't get behind them. This attribute is particularly obvious when facing challenges.

Most Inspirational Leaders are in charge of or influence power, but are not "Preachers." They are "Doers" who guide others to succeed. Inspirational Leaders can move people to see things from different points of view. They rebound from defeats and inspire their organizations to greatness when others throw in the towel. Overall, Inspirational Leaders make great employees.

SECRET ONE: DEVELOP A CLEAR PATH TO BEING AN INSPIRATIONAL LEADER THAT REFLECTS YOUR IDENTITY

To be an Inspirational Leader, do not start out with the question, "What do I want?" Ask instead, "What needs to be done?" Then ask, "What can and should I do to make a difference?"

You can become an Inspirational Leader by fighting the temptation to do things that are *popular* rather than right. Also, resist the urge to do things that are petty, mean or unprofessional.

It is important to know yourself. Does your leadership style represent your identity as you perceive it? Does it represent your identity as others perceive it? As you wish it were perceived?

Fit your leadership approach to your strengths. If you are clear and genuine with your identity, you will attract and retain those who resonate with your identity. People want to work with others who have clarity about who they are.

Submit yourself to the "mirror test." Is the person you see in the mirror in the morning the kind of person you believe in, want to be, and respect?

Inspirational Leaders perform rigorous self-evaluation. Ask yourself, "Do I accept responsibility when something goes wrong or do I blame others? Am I good at building teams and motivating team members? Do I think strategically rather than get sidetracked by the 'idea of the week'?"

> **A leader looks out the window, not in the mirror.**

A leader doesn't follow someone else's footprints. Instead, he or she carves their own path. A leader doesn't look for the light at the end of the tunnel, but focuses on what is at hand and on achieving set goals. Instead of flaunting his or her title, a leader uses their position and knowledge to help others. A leader looks for ways to help employees improve and better themselves. Rather than taking credit for success, a leader celebrates everyone involved in achieving that success. A leader is not arrogant, but is confident and helpful.

SECRET TWO: GOALS AND VALUES

A Shared Organization Vision and Core Values

Joseph Murphy once said, "We go where our vision is," which sums up the importance of a shared Organization Vision. To achieve this, start by instilling the Organization Vision Statement in employees. Do this by reiterating the Vision in every meeting and frequently in communications.

Clear Core Values make leadership decisions much easier. High-Impact Managers make sure that Core Values are instilled in their organizations by citing them as part of each critical decision and consistently talking about them in their communications.

Use Goals to Inspire

Inspirational Leaders track and monitor their subordinates' activities to insure they make progress in their responsibilities. It is not enough if subordinates say, after engagement with you, "I feel good, I'm inspired, I'm motivated." which is great. It's more important that they show something concrete they have gotten as a result of your leadership.

Goals don't need to be big, but they must *inspire*. A department chair once told me, "I want my department to have the lowest customer return in the organization's history." This goal was *inspiring* to him.

Think about any one goal you have right now for you subordinates. Why do you want it? What will happen when they achieve it? Will it give them any of the following: comfort, pride, balance, peace, harmony, security, etc.?

Use a Rallying Goal to inspire employees and get them motivated. The Rallying Goal should require most employees of the organization to contribute in order to achieve it. This goal can't be revised and should be attainable within a three-year timetable (preferably sooner).

> "Leadership is the act of arousing, engaging, and satisfying the motives of followers in an environment of conflict, competition or change that results in the follwers taking a course of action toward a mutually shared vision."
> – Ken Blanchard

There are several mistakes to avoid when creating a goal. It shouldn't be stated in a negative way. The goal will be uninspiring if it is too reasonable and if there is no deadline for achieving it. Be sure to word the goal as a direct command, and don't have a "Plan B" to back it up. Having a

> **Teams aligned to goals inspired by a leader routinely outperform their competitors. Some studies report the difference at 200% or more.**

Plan B makes the goal less inspiring, because employees think, "Well, if we don't successfully achieve the goal, there's always a backup plan."

Don't Confuse Activity with Achievement

It's about getting results, not just working hard. You can work harder and harder every day but not achieve the right results, which is why it is important to understand the difference between activity and achievement. Avoid creating goals or objectives that are activity-focused, not achievement-focused. Employees must see how their achievements will lead to reaching a desired goal or objective.

Now let's think about how you say things. Don't ask," What objective do you *want* to achieve or what objective do you think you're going to work on this month?" Make a commitment by asking, "What objective are you committed to achieving?"

You Need Wins

One organization leader said, "If I'm going to get renewed focus on these 30-day goals, I am going to talk about multiple

> **Help employees focus on achieving the goal without a "Plan B" in the back of their minds.**

ways of getting there before floating out another goal to the group."

It's not about How Inspirational You Sound

Inspirational leadership skills are not dependent on how inspiring you sound, but rather on clearly identifying goals on which the team needs to focus.

Enthusiasm

As an inspiring party, you need to access that part of you that "talks up a good game," gets other people excited and rallied around a vision, and then turn them loose to achieve great results, because they believe they can. In this role, you're going to say such things as, "Let's go for it and we will hit the goal."

In this role, you don't tell your subordinates specifically what to do, but rather focus on inspiring them to reach for the goals.

How can you inspire creative thinking among employees? Ask for out-of-the-box ideas. It is a myth that most fresh, creative ideas come from new hires and that long tenure creates stale thinking. Inspirational Leaders create the mood to move people to do what must be accomplished. In addition, they offer a "teachable" point of view that is the foundation for their coaching.

> You work inspirationally through other people. It's all about them and how they feel.

Subordinates are also inspired by your interest in how they would do things. One of my favorite questions for getting a subordinate's thoughts on improving organizations results is to ask, "If you were the key decision-maker in the organization, what would you do right now?" and "If you could wave a magic wand and change it any way you want, how would it be?"

Celebrate the Accomplishments

Inspirational Leaders are engaged and passionate about helping their employees discover their talents. They help make their people successful. Have a plan for celebrating employee accomplishments.

Inspirational Leaders make the process enjoyable by celebrating specific milestones and finding win-win situations that are good for them, as well as others, and serves a greater good.

Create a brand affiliation for your organization. Give out logo ware like shirts, hats, coats, pens, notebooks, mouse pads, etc. to employees. Create a team loyalty system that includes team rewards and recognition for accomplishments. Even create organization rituals. All of these things will help instill a sense of purpose in employees and meaning in the work they do.

SECRET THREE: UNDERSTANDING ROLES

Employees Need to Understand Their Roles

Inspirational Leaders value product/service quality, employee empowerment and reducing bureaucracy. They recognize that employees need to understand what you want them to do regarding any plan of action, as well as how you are going to be involved, if at all. Your team needs to understand what they are specifically accountable for doing.

Understanding the Inspirational Leader's Role in Team Meetings

Inspirational Leaders never scream at employees or allow subordinates to yell at them or at other managers. This stifles the desire to follow management.

Energy Game in Group Presentations

Inspirational Leadership is very much an energy game for everybody. Just as when you're in front of a group or about to give a speech, that first couple of minutes sets the tone for the event. Prepare yourself to make sure that you're ready to do it with energy. When a session starts, act as if you've been going at it for ten or fifteen minutes, not just starting to ramp up your energy. Clear your head and do whatever else you need to do to be at your highest energy level when you start your group communication.

If you are among the many who fear speaking before groups, then work on your presentation skills. Take a Dale Carnegie program or join a local club, like Toastmasters, in which all the members have to publicly speak before the other members.

Make Timely Decisions

Making decisions in a timely manner is very important so your employees do not feel they are wasting their time and resent you for it. When discussions are getting to a point where progress is not being made toward resolving things, move on. Shine the focus back on the matter under discussion.

After someone has expressed their view, ask other employees what ideas they have regarding the view and suggestions to make it better. This sets a tone in which you appreciate the idea just expressed while at the same time asking people to challenge it by asking for improvements. This approach works particularly well with team members who avoid conflict and don't share their views.

SECRET FOUR: CONNECT WITH YOUR EMPLOYEES AND MAKE THEM FEEL SPECIAL

Emotional Meaning

Instill meaning in your subordinates, such as emotional meaning. How can we reach our goal? How can you make this happen? That's about the *why* and the *how*. There will be multiple ways to realize an objective. What does this mean emotionally to them?

Developing these Inspirational Leadership skills will give you the ability to motivate your employees to produce exceptional results and feel more fulfilled than ever before. You don't have to be an exciting motivational communicator to be outstanding as an Inspirational Leader. In fact, most are not great motivational communicators. But they do have certain traits in common, which you can make part of your management style.

First, when making a public commitment about what results will be, give emotional leverage to those to whom this is communicated.

The CEO of a manufacturing company called all his employees in to a company-wide meeting to share his declaration that the company would grow from a $1,500,000 company to a $5,000,000 company within three years. He did a wonderful presentation with graphs and a PowerPoint presentation and "sold the sizzle," basically guaranteeing the results. Unfortunately, making the declaration almost immediately hurt his image as an Inspirational Leader because few employees believed the results were truly attainable. His image was further hurt when sales regressed over the period of time when they were supposed to hit the $5,000,000 mark.

The emotional component is actually the driver of inspiration. Then you must find the vehicle that fits the environment—actually, multiple vehicles—in order to have a viable failsafe plan.

Inspire Best by Customizing to the Behavior of Subordinates

Try to understand your subordinates' natural and adapted styles. Their natural styles are where they will put their greatest energy and find the least stress.

Discuss strengths with employees and things they are passionate about. For example, Jerome had spent decades in sales management, but had never achieved great success. One day, I was at a planning team meeting in which Jerome's boss, brought up how poor Jerome's sales team results had been for the last year. His boss (who was also president of the organization) felt that Jerome's winning personality and thorough understanding of the benefits of what his team was selling, should have made him a guaranteed winner in the selling game.

> **Promise only what you know can be achieved.**

I asked the president if anyone in the organization had ever asked Jerome if he had a genuine passion for sales. The vice president of the organization volunteered to discuss the subject with Jerome. In this discussion, Jerome confessed he never enjoyed his job. He was able to do it to a certain level, but he had never truly succeeded because the passion he needed was missing.

The vice president worked with Jerome to uncover his passions. Within 30 days, Jerome's role in the organization was restructured to one where he was no longer required to manage the sales staff, an activity he dreaded. His new role as Director of Training took advantage of his institutional knowledge,

passion for training, and interacting with people. Jerome's career
move took him from being an
unsuccessful sales manager to
being a very important cog in the
organization's success.

> **"Nourishing relationships has a beneficial impact on our health, while toxic ones can act like a slow poison in our bodies." – Daniel Goldman, *Social Intelligence***

Ease in Discussing Personal with Subordinates

Inspirational Leaders feel
comfortable discussing personal as well as organization high-
lights. Walk through what you want your subordinate to do
with your guidance, as well as if and when they are going to
get it done. Make a commitment to specific action plans with
timeframes. This helps get something accomplished by the end
of your conversation.

Break routine and do something like go to lunch with the
subordinate. This kind of relationship-building adds value to
reinforce what you are inspiring your subordinates to achieve.
For example, if you want to develop a casual acquaintance,
arrange it around meeting for a cup of coffee in the morning,
tack lunch onto a meeting, or grab a drink at the end of
the day.

While nourishing relationships, it is important to maintain
a line between coworkers and social friends, as this is hard to
change once the process begins. Also, keep in mind that any
perception of a double standard or "protected employee" is a
disaster for employee morale.

Make Employees Feel Special

Inspirational Leaders make employees feel special. Walk
around to where the employees work and talk to them on their

turf. Do not start talking to employees right before quitting time or first thing in the morning. Each day, decide who you will talk to and what you will talk about for tomorrow. "Get out there, ask them if there's anything you can do to help." – Robert Townsend, *Further up the Organization*

> **Make employees feel special by having them feel like they are part of something important.**

Inspirational Leaders' Influence on Organization Morale

Good organization morale is important for getting a positive view of you as an Inspirational Leader. One way to help bring about good morale is to keep discussions from sinking to the level of hurtful, personal attacks.

The passion of successful performers can be defeated by the pessimism of poor performers. Protect good people from negative people. Find and control the "Office Thermostat." Do not tolerate bitter, cynical, sarcastic employees.

Give Feedback on How They Are Doing

If you have a subordinate who takes no notes, has no capture system or doesn't perform very well, then you could send them an outline of accomplishments and challenges over the last few months. Say, "I'll shoot you an email with some of the things that I've captured. If you see anything you want to add, change or delete, let me know, and we'll talk about it. Why don't we set aside two hours (or an hour and a half) to look at how things are going?" This will help motivate your subordinate to get more involved.

SECRET FIVE: USE TEAMS AND SHARE CREDIT

Inspirational Leaders Use and Inspire Project Teams

It's common to assign a small number of people to work together toward a common goal with the responsibility for success being that of the team, rather than an individual. Typically, these working groups or project teams are established for a specific

> "People become really quite remarkable when they start thinking that they can do things. When they believe in themselves they have the first secret of success."
> – Norman Vincent Peale

project, operate for a short period of time and are disbanded when the project is over. Often, employees on the team retain their functional department responsibilities. It's common for no support staff to be assigned. Communication and project documentation may be informal.

Inspirational Leaders identify where a team or work group can fit for best results by asking, "In which area or project? How many would be on the team?" Then list the members and their attributes. By using a project team, you can draw on a broader mix of skills, experience, and know-how and gain greater flexibility (it is not a structured group, decisions can be made quickly).

Inspirational Leaders must make sure that with each step forward, the project team is celebrated. Inspirational Leaders use team performance goals to energize teams (results can be seen more immediately). A key objective is developing a team discipline towards achieving goals, as well as individual accountability to each other.

Be sensitive to the frequency of meeting times based on the urgency of the goal. How much work needs to be accomplished?

> **The desire to not let each other down can be very motivating.**

How many "normal" work hours can be "sacrificed" for the project? A good acronym to remember when working with a team is TORI: Trust, Openness, Realization, Interdependence.

Inspiration hopefully will bring about real enthusiasm and personal commitment to performance results. Performance results should lead to rewards.

Share the Bigger Picture

Your team members need to understand your view of a bigger reality, not just the reality involved in discussing a particular point. Develop a pattern of communicating with your employees in a very comprehensive manner so they can get excited because they see how the projects they are working on fit into the bigger picture of the vision for the organization.

It is better for your team members to understand more of a situation than less. I like my team members to understand why I want to do something, rather than just what it is that I want to be done.

> **The more employees know, the more likely they are to be creative with their decisions and have a clear path of how to make decisions relating to a topic.**

Something else takes place when you share more information with your employees; you're likely to engage with them more emotionally. Those employees who see things the same way you do are more likely to come to views and decisions resembling yours and to do so more quickly.

Your employees need to feel free to ask questions of everybody on the team, including you as the Key Decision-Maker.

They may disagree with any team member's view, but need to give them reasons why they disagree.

Inspirational Leaders Get Great Results from Project Teams

Inspirational Leaders get great results by establishing urgency and direction, as well as selecting employee skills and skill potential. Creating rules for behavior and immediate performance-oriented tasks as goals while challenging employees with facts and information also yields great results. Have employees spend as much time together as possible and provide the team with positive feedback. Understand the strengths and weaknesses of employees and the roles they actually fill. Inspirational Leaders form the project teams, monitor how the team operates, and make sure the team is performing well together.

Vary your approach to inspiring a team, based on the team project or concept. The key decision is who should lead the group. The chosen leader may change if a major conflict occurs between the team and the leader.

Inspirational Leaders should keep the purpose, goals, and approach for employee activities meaningful. They build commitment and confidence while helping develop the skills of employees. They create opportunities for employees to do genuine work, not just serve as a figurehead. They celebrate small wins and inject information about each win, small or large.

At times, use an outside trained facilitator and change the team's membership, including the leader.

Look out for "group-think," resulting in the critical thinking process being suspended by your team because of:

- Too much cohesiveness and conformity
- The illusion of invulnerability

- Collective rationalization
- "Mindguards" (protective individuals who deter non-group thinking and "outside thinking")
- Direct negative pressure applied to dissenters
- Self-censorship
- Illusion of unanimity

Inspirational Leaders Share the Credit

A flock of geese was getting ready to fly south for the winter. One goose had a broken wing and couldn't fly, so he found a stick and asked two other geese if they would each put an end of the stick in their beaks as they flew south. His plan was to hold onto the middle of the stick with his beak. The geese agreed to help him. The three lined up, put the stick in their beaks and took off on their flight. Later in the journey, another goose noticed the two geese towing the goose with the broken wing and complimented them on their teamwork.

"What a great idea! Whose idea was it, anyway?" he asked.

The goose with the broken wing immediately piped up, "It was my idea!"

By opening his beak to talk, he let go of the stick and fell to his death.

Many organization leaders and managers tend to view things in an "I" rather than a "We" perspective. Taking all the credit—or assuming an "I" perspective—is a leadership weakness. The chances of an organization reaching its full potential are much greater if the owner does not take all of the credit.

It is counterproductive to adopt an "I" perspective and turn people off. Many organizations have been held back from their potential, and, in some cases, even destroyed, because of an owner who took credit for everything.

I learned personally how counterproductive an "I" mentality can be while serving as an employee at The May Department Stores Company. The day before a major committee meeting, I presented the officer to whom I reported with a rather novel approach to solving a problem the company faced. I had spent a lot of time and energy coming up with what I considered to be the best solution to the problem.

The officer and I spent hours discussing the proposal. At the committee meeting the next day, he presented my proposal as his own idea. I was livid, but because of the practical factors involved, I could not object during the meeting.

Afterwards, I walked into his office and asked how he could have taken credit for my idea. "We are a team," he replied, "and as the head of the team, it is best if shown as my idea." There was no further room for discussion on the topic; it was simply the way it was.

Prior to that incident, I had gone out of my way to always talk him up within the company. After this occurrence, I never again made any effort to help him beyond doing my job.

SECRET SIX: ACCOUNTABILITY

Inspirational Leaders Are Self-Accountable

With many leaders, there typically exists a lack of self-accountability because they believe they are not accountable to anyone beyond themselves. As a result, when a leader announces a plan to do something and it doesn't happen, it is unlikely any members of their team will continue to hold the leader in high regard.

Inspirational Leaders Walk the Walk

Many managers talk a great game, but their actions don't

follow their words. If you tell your employees to work hard on a project, but show up late and leave early yourself, you are not inspiring them. Your subordinates are watching you closely. Like it or not, your actions and words teach volumes about leadership.

Inspirational Leaders speak with bold clarity. They earn respect as a leader by choosing their words with care.

Inspirational Leaders don't make rash decisions. They finalize their decisions only after gathering sufficient facts and weighing all of the options. They closely detail everyone's responsibilities and then mobilize employees to get started. Inspirational Leaders encourage their employees to establish a personal work-related goal or goals, a plan to achieve the goal and action steps that ensure they know what must be done to achieve the goal.

SECRET SEVEN: DO NOT AVOID CONFLICT

Inspirational Leaders do not Avoid Conflict

Be on the lookout for employees who come to work each day and seem to have no interest in what's happening outside their own department. This type of attitude may seem harmless, but it can have a very negative effect. Humans are curious by nature and your employees should express some interest in what's going on in the organization. A lack of interest is a warning signal that the employee is probably not highly motivated and will likely operate at much lower than reasonable levels of efficiency.

An organization owner, whom I will call Joe, had an employee who consistently worked a few hours and then would sneak out early via the back stairwell. The employee didn't return clients' phone calls or follow through with his job responsibilities.

Joe rationalized that he should avoid a confrontation because the employee was achieving some sales and, after all, "his replacement could be worse." Joe was aggravated by the situation, but again he rationalized, "Better to deal with the devil you know than the devil you don't." In reality, the problem was that Joe did not like conflict, so he avoided it. As a result, Joe's organization never generated outstanding profits.

Many organization owners have kept employees on staff long after it became apparent that they could not handle their responsibilities in the desired manner.

Do you regularly shy away from resolving difficulties with others in order to avoid conflict? Have you ever delayed, or put off indefinitely, firing someone who plainly should be fired? If so, your avoidance of conflict is a weakness that you must acknowledge or it will keep you from reaching your dreams.

Employees who are "Meddlers"

The world is full of employees who are "meddlers." The meddler often works by zeroing in on a new employee. He will say that he is only helping the new employee get acquainted with the way things are done. Such action may be appreciated at first, but eventually you need to see through the façade and call them on the truth.

The meddler will also interfere with experienced employees by voluntarily jumping in "to give a hand" whenever they see an opportunity. They may claim that the other employee was falling behind and that they were just trying to help, but just as with the example above, a meddler's true motivation comes from a much different direction.

A meddler can hold any position in the organization, from front-desk receptionist to top-level management. Unless you stand up to the meddler, he will have a detrimental effect on the way others work, and ultimately will hurt your chances of realizing your plans.

So, how do you handle an employee who wants to help others when they don't want the help?

The difficulty in taking assertive action to halt the meddling lies in the fact that meddlers often mean no harm. They view themselves as being sensitive and compassionate, even though others see them in quite a different light. Therefore, redirecting the meddler's "well-meaning" energy must be approached delicately.

> **"A king does not abide within his tent while his men bleed and die upon the field."**
> **– Steven Pressman, Gates of Fire**

First, try to understand what's going on in the meddler's mind. They probably feel a real desire to help people, so you can assume that helping people is something that is very important to them. The meddler quite likely does not mean to come across as a know-it-all; they are simply looking for acceptance.

The best assertive action to take is to reinforce how important they are to the organization, but to note they create problems with their meddling. They must understand that employees do not want (and often resent) their help.

Another type of meddler is one who thrives on offering unwelcome advice to co-workers regarding their personal lives. This type of meddler is also capable of creating problems within an organization.

Turn a Threat into an Opportunity

Danger is implicit in any crisis, but within any crisis there is also the opportunity for constructive action. Threats are based on circumstances over which we have no control, so there is no real way to stop them from happening. However, learning to recognize the patterns and signs that point toward potential threats allows us to prepare tactics for handling and reacting to a threat if one should occur.

Inspirational Leaders lead the charge during tough organization times. They handle stressful situations without losing focus and direction. They turn the working atmosphere into a "Red Badge of Courage" and don't overreact to individual events. Leadership is about coping with change and complexity.

RATE YOURSELF

On a scale of 1–10, rate yourself on the following characteristics common to Inspirational Leaders:

__ High morale, motivation and productivity
__ Promotes strong teamwork and cross-functional cooperation by all employees in the organization regardless of the department in which they work
__ Strong loyalty to the organization
__ Builds employee trust of organization
__ Provides clarity of mission
__ Empowers employees
__ Shows high integrity in the workplace
__ Develops strong trust relationships
__ Creates effective systems and processes
__ Focuses on customer/client satisfaction
__ Encourages effective 360-degree communications

___ Committed to learning and skill development

___ Emphasizes recruiting and retaining outstanding employees

___ Displays a high degree of adaptability

___ Shows high accountability standards

___ Demonstrates support for innovation

CONCLUSION

To what degree do you think you play the inspiring role? Are there opportunities you can take advantage of, which you aren't already doing?

HABIT 3

High Impact Coaching

The time you spend coaching employees of your organization—whether those who directly report to you or those who report to your direct reports—will help them increase their impact on your business. You will be assisting these employees to perform better within the confines of your organizational objectives and, in turn, assisting your organization to perform better. It will help them move to a level they may not have been able to reach in the past.

Using your coaching skills helps employees become more productive in a wide range of impact areas. The most obvious areas include increased revenue, lowered

> **Through coaching, a lot can be accomplished by developing selected employees.**

costs and improved organizational morale/culture. In addition, this coaching will bring about micro-positive impact all the way down to employees work habits (meeting deadlines, his or her quality of work, etc.).

Coaching employees can create lasting change and impact

their lives. It also allows you to deepen relationships with your employees.

The benefits of your coaching skills will be meaningful whether the employee you are coaching is performing poorly or successfully in certain areas. Coaching can be provided through one-on-one interaction or group interaction. It is effective in communications, goal-setting, strategic planning and other areas.

> **Mastering High-Impact Manager coaching skills will build rapport and deepen relationship with your employees.**

Remember, it is the employee, not the coach, who should make decisions on how to address the situation.

COACHING HAS MOVING TARGETS

One reason coaching is so challenging for most managers is that it requires them to be dealing with the psychology of others— often, a moving target. Sometimes, the personalities of people you are coaching changes a lot. Dealing with this uncertainty requires flexibility.

ROOTS OF COACHING

The term "coaching" has its roots in team and sports activities. Historically, a coach is someone who has performed that sport at a high level. The coach guides the players to their highest possible level of execution.

Coaching employees in organizations conceptually involves the same elements as that of coaching sports teams. Ultimately, the objective is to win.

DIFFERENT TYPES OF ROLES

One of the tenets of coaching roles is asking questions to help the employee come to their own decision.

BE SELECTIVE AS TO WHOM YOU COACH

Because coaching takes up time, be selective when deciding whom to work with in a coaching role. I coach employees with the potential to make major contributions to our organization. The employees I select have both high potential and a desire to learn from the coaching process.

ESTABLISH GROUND RULES BEFORE STARTING COACHING ACTIVITIES

When discussing with your selected employee your willingness to provide coaching, also discuss how you expect to interact in your coaching role. Explain how this relationship differs from managing an employee. Then ask something that shows whether he or she wants to be coached. "In order for you to get the most out of this relationship, I need to know if you want me to be your Coach. If your answer is no, it's OK. So, do you want me to coach you?"

WHEN AND WHERE

Typically, I do not schedule meetings specifically for coaching employees. I do the coaching very informally, by walking into the employee's office and opening with a question like, "Is there anything I can help you with?" Often I find that the coaching conversation is most effectively handled if you and the employee share a meal together.

Some High-Impact Managers, on the other hand, prefer a formal meeting scheduled at a specific time and conducted in the Coach's office. For example, the chief technology officer of one company schedules coaching meetings months in advance; he meets with employees two to four times a month, with each meeting scheduled for 30-60 minutes.

For most types of coaching, you must initially agree on being on time for coaching meetings, coming prepared for the meeting and staying present with focus during the meeting.

The "where" should be someplace you can meet privately in person. This isn't always possible. At times you will need to work with employees distantly located. Use Skype-type video communications for long-distance coaching. You can use Skype-type communications on all subjects, as long as it does not require you to do physical work.

Part of the appeal of coaching is in-person interaction. You don't want to make video coaching the norm if your employee is located near you. But being a virtual coach can be powerfully effective, so don't rule out the idea.

COACHING AGENDA

While there may be structure and sometimes an informal agenda in your mind of what you want to do when coaching a particular employee at a particular time, your coaching is generally not very structured. In fact, you often will not be able to predict the direction the interaction is going to take.

COACHING SKILLS

Let's look at the coaching skills needed to make your employees more effective and see how you can use them.

COACHING SKILL #1: BE SUPPORTIVE

You need to be supportive, understanding and non-critical when discussing factors that led to the problems the employee faces. Provide positive support and feedback while helping the employee recognize ways in which she can improve the effectiveness of her responsibilities in the business.

Employees have within themselves most of the resources needed to answer (or find the answer) to the challenge or opportunity they face. Your role as a coach is to help them tap into these resources.

The coach facilitates the employee's goals and desires, helping him and helps strategize what is needed for the attainment of specific objectives.

The focus is on the needs of the employee. Therefore, the employee is the "end user," or beneficiary, of your coaching services. You are coaching your employee to achieve the employee's work related objectives and to serve as a vehicle for attaining greater levels of personal fulfillment at work.

COACHING SKILL #2: HELP EMPLOYEES DEVELOP PROCESSES, PROTOCOLS AND PROCEDURES

Help your employees build structure for addressing future, similar challenges in their jobs with a focus on processes, protocols and procedures. You want them to see that the structure moving forward will help them be more efficient the next time they encounter a similar situation. This will be easier with some employees because of their natural behaviors, rather than others whose behavior styles are a bad fit with structure. Try to get them to enjoy the structure needed for operating most effectively.

While coaching one manager, I realized that the problem he was discussing had been addressed several times in the past. We explored those attempts and he decided to write a step-by-step protocol of how things should be handled when these types of situations occur in the future.

COACHING SKILL #3: IDENTIFY THE REAL PROBLEM

As a Coach, you will need to identify the real problem on which you should focus. Sometimes the problem is not what the employee is telling you. Often, there is an underlying psychological factor and that is the *real* problem. In your coaching role, identify psychological factors or habits that led to the employee's problem in the first place. Only then can you work on actually solving the problem.

Use your coaching skills to help employees discover what is stopping them from getting what they want in their work life. In order to do this, you need to understand the root causes of the problems being faced. The cliché is true: "Healthy roots bring about healthy foliage and fruit." You can't coach employees at the best level if you can't identify the root cause of the problems. Ultimately, your coaching should help employees acquire the mental processing ability to make decisions or take actions without your help.

COACHING SKILL #4: ASK QUESTIONS

Coaching doesn't require that you dictate actions for the employee to take, but instead use your interpersonal skills to help the employee with the thinking needed to make a good decision on his or her own. This usually involves asking lots of questions. For example, an engineer facilitating his team's full-day meeting focused on creating a business plan for a new product. He asked questions and gave advice at times, but was not there to write the plan himself.

> **Deal first with root causes of a problem. "Healthy roots results in healthy foliage and healthy trees."**

One reason to ask questions is to further the employee's self-awareness. Your goal is to facilitate your employee's processing of a particular issue by asking questions the employee has not asked on their own. By offering a neutral and objective perspective, you can play an integral role in your employee's discovery process.

Be sure to ask probing and clarifying questions as well. Probing questions drive to the core of the issue. Clarifying questions seek understanding. These questions come from a place of curiosity and do not seek to challenge the employee.

Ask questions beginning with What, Who, When, Why and How. For example, when your employee discusses something he or she needs to do, ask, "Why does this have to be done now rather than next year?" Also ask, "How does this relate to the rest of the job?"

COACHING SKILL #5: SHARE STORIES

Another effective coaching technique is to share stories of your own experiences, whether the outcome was good or bad. For example, an employee of a VP had an HR issue dealing with her second in command who had come into her office to say, "Oh, by the way, I'm not going to work Fridays anymore." The employee asked, "What should I do with this?" The VP did not tell her what to do. Instead, she shared several stories of similar situations, how she had handled them and the consequences that ensued. The employee drew from these stories to determine the course of action she should take.

Another benefit of sharing your experiences is that, hopefully, this will lead the employee to tap into similar types of experiences. In this way, they may avoid making certain mistakes made along the way by others.

COACHING SKILL #6: REQUIRE EMPLOYEE REPORTING BACK WHAT IS DONE ABOUT A SITUATION

Coaching employees can be a great investment of your time. However, it will not be worthwhile unless the selected employees are receptive to your involvement. A coached employee should give you a clear commitment that he or she will report back to you about what they do about particular situations. Commitment to accountability is a must in order to know if your coaching is getting results that justify your commitment of time.

Be clear that reporting back what the employee decides to do about a situation is a requirement of the coaching process. This factor is often referred to as "coaching accountability."

COACHING SKILL #7: ADDRESSING EMPLOYEE NEED FOR SIGNIFICANCE OR SECURITY

The two most dominant emotions that must be managed are a need for *certainty* and a need for *significance*. Certainty is the emotion or the feeling of being in our comfort zone. Our need for significance relates to being successful at what we do.

You will need to deal with these emotions on a regular basis. They create forces that affect virtually every problem you face with your employees. When they bring up problems, ask yourself whether they are feeling uncertain or insignificant, or both. Determine what you can do to help them achieve either significance or certainty, so they can move forward.

COACHING SKILL #8: ADJUST HOW YOU COACH BASED UPON NATURAL BEHAVIOR STYLES

Know your own natural behavior style and be aware of the natural behavior styles of those you coach. You may need to adapt your style to best interact with an employee, based on his or her behavior style.

Generally, there are four different behavioral styles—Dominance, Influence, Steadiness and Compliance. A high dominance personality places emphasis on accomplishing results, keeping the bottom line in mind and acting with a great deal of confidence. A high influence personality seeks to persuade others using their personality; they are open and optimistic by nature. A high steadiness personality is very cooperative, sincere and dependable. A high compliance personality places emphasis on quality, accuracy, expertise and competence. So, for example, if you are a high dominance personality coaching a high compliance personality, you may need to slow down and give your employee more facts and figures than might otherwise be necessary.

COACHING SKILL #9: ENCOURAGE CHALLENGING CONVERSATIONS

You want your employees to challenge you if you are not moving in the direction they think you should go. Encourage employees to share with you why their own life or professional experiences lead them to disagree with the direction in which you are leading them, so long as the discussion takes place in a positive way.

COACHING SKILL #10: HELP EMPLOYEES RECOGNIZE "UNCONSCIOUS INCOMPETENCE"

Employees are likely to resist your coaching methods because they *don't know what they don't know.* This is the state of being incompetent in an area, but not recognizing their incompetence. The skills or techniques for coaching your employees toward achievement in these areas won't work until you can create an awareness of factors that must be considered, and which don't show up on their radar.

COACHING SKILL #11: UNDERSTAND, BUT DO NOT DWELL ON THE PAST

Keep your discussions focused on the present and future. While a past experience might be referred to, do not let your employee focus or dwell on it. Begin with the present and build toward the future.

Coaching deals strictly with the challenges, issues, opportunities and learning prospects in the present. You want the employee to determine a specific course of future action in order to attain the desired objective. If the employee has emotional issues that originated in the past and still haunt him or her today, suggest that they consult a professional therapist who can provide the help they need. You can still continue to coach the employee even if she or he engages someone else for therapeutic support.

COACHING SKILL #12: PROVIDE FEEDBACK, BUT DON'T DEFINE THE GOAL

Coaching requires a mutual conversation during which you provide feedback and direction about focusing thoughts and behaviors in productive and affirming ways. A Coach does not define the goal of the coaching; the employee does. Establish the topics for coaching by asking questions such as, "What would like to discuss today?", "How can I best support you?" and "How can I best support in achieving objectives?"

COACHING SKILL #13: COMMUNICATING YOU CARE

Carefully select the verbiage that best communicates your understanding to the employee in a way that provides encouragement, rapport, respect, trust, cooperation and support. This is helped by the appropriate use of paraphrasing and offering respectful, reflective comments. Also, your body language should be consistent with this message of caring that you want your communication to convey.

COACHING SKILL #14: GET DEEPER UNDERSTANDING OF YOUR EMPLOYEE

You will do a better job with your coaching activities if you have a deeper understanding of your employee than you may already have. Ask non-threatening questions to help you acquire this understanding and help employees a gain new perspective on themselves. The following questions can lead you to this deeper understanding:

- Who are you at your best?
- If you were coaching you, how would you coach you right now?
- When you step outside of yourself and watch yourself in action, what do you see?
- What was the toughest circumstance you overcame in your life and how did you overcome it?

- What was the toughest circumstance you overcame in your work career and how did you overcome it?
- Who among organization personnel would take pleasure in your success?
- Who do you think would take pleasure in your failure?
- Who gets under your skin?
- Why do they get under your skin?

COACHING SKILL #15: ADDRESS AND THEN GET PAST VENTING BY YOUR EMPLOYEE

During coaching, it's common for an employee to vent about certain subjects. This isn't all bad, since the reality is until he or she releases certain emotions, they may remain stuck and blocked to your help. Get this out of the way by asking, "What's bothering you that you need to get off your chest once and for all?" or "Let it rip and then we can move on."

COACHING SKILL #16: REVISIT OF SIGNIFICANT LIFE- AND WORK-RELATED EVENTS AND ISSUES SINCE THE LAST MEETING

Ask your employee, "Give me the highlight reel on your major stories since we last spoke." Push them on their performance since the last meeting. Ask, "How does not making progress help you achieve your stated goal?"

COACHING SKILL #17: SHARE YOUR OBSERVATIONS

Say something such as, "I notice patterns that come up that may be holding your back. Let's bring those observations up now so we can discuss them. Is that OK?" (Await acknowledgement.)

COACHING SKILL #18: MOVE EMPLOYEE TO CLEAR COMMITMENT TO DO SOMETHING

Ask, "What" questions such as, "What specifically must happen to make the accomplishment of the objective a '10'? What is the impact if you don't get the desired results? What is the cost of not taking action? What will be the benefit of taking action?"

Results from your Coaching activities will ultimately be judged by what your employee does *in between* meetings. One way to help get clarity is to say things such as:

- "Let me repeat what I heard you say."
- "May I summarize/paraphrase what I just heard?"
- "Do I understand you correctly when you said ... (repeat what he/she just said)?"
- "Will you please elaborate on that point?"

COACHING SKILL #19: OBSERVE AND ACTIVELY LISTEN

When acting in a Coach role, be fully present and in the moment with your employee. This way, you can observe and actively listen to any spoken and unspoken clues the employee offers. Subtle body and verbal language cues reveal the core reason of the employee's challenge and why the employee may find himself or herself stuck. Look for meaning in gestures, voice qualities, changes in word choice, general discomfort and other unusual things about his or her emotional state.

COACHING SKILL #20: ASK THE SAME QUESTION IN MORE THAN ONE WAY IF YOU HAVE DOUBTS AS TO SINCERITY

An employee's initial answer, particularly a knee-jerk response, may *not* be the true answer. If so, ask the same question in a different way. If you don't get the same answer, ask the question yet a different way. A series of three similar answers means you are most likely hearing the truth. If not, continue to ask questions until you get to the real answers.

COACHING SKILL #21: CELEBRATE PROGRESS TO DATE

Help the employee enjoy the journey. Celebrate each success, big or little, whenever an achievement takes place.

COACHING SKILL #22: APPEAL TO EACH OF THE THREE OBSERVABLE SENSES

Appeal to each of the three observable senses (Visual – see, Auditory – hear and Kinesthetic – feel) that are used by your employees to process things. You appeal to the visual sense of your employee by showing them things, whether articles, graphs, memos, etc. You appeal to the hearing sense by using words and tone of voice. When appealing to the kinesthetic sense, use a hands-on approach. If you are using an Excel proforma model, for example, have the person physically do what is needed to use the computerized model, rather than you doing the keyboarding.

COACHING SKILL #23: MATCH AND MIRROR TO CREATE FACE-TO-FACE RAPPORT

We are more relaxed and open with people who are like us. You can reduce barriers by doing what is referred to as "matching and mirroring." This involves matching and mirroring in the following three different areas:

Match and mirror the employee physiology, such as sitting and standing positions, postures, hand gestures, pace of movements, leaning (back or forward), crossing or uncrossing of legs, arms and proximity.

Appeal to the hearing sense of the person by matching and mirroring voice qualities, such as volume, pace, tempo and inflection. Match and mirror the employee's emotional speaking intensity by matching the *intensity*, not the *emotion*. Finally, match and mirror words, such as repeated words, key phrases, words that seem to be emotionally charged and personal / regional 'jargon' (y'all, really?).

COACHING SKILL #24: GET BUY-IN BY USING TAGGED QUESTIONS TO INFLUENCE ANSWERS

Make a statement with a question "tagged" onto the end:
- Nice job of financial modeling, isn't it?
- Jane does a great job in customer service, wouldn't you agree?

COACHING SKILL #25: MOVE THE EMPLOYEE TO DEEPER LEVELS OF PROCESSING OF AN ISSUE

Get the employee to *think*, instead of just reacting. Bring the employee to a higher level of learning, thereby taking them to "unconscious competence." Consider what you can say to give the person a new perspective to an issue.

The following are examples of what to say to "drill down deeper:"

- Tell me more about the <problem>.
- What caused the <problem> to happen?
- How long has this <problem> gone on?

- How does that make you feel?
- What have you tried to fix the <the problem>?
- How did it work? Why didn't it work?
- How much longer can you afford this <problem> to go on?
- At what point would this <problem> be considered a crisis?
- What are you planning to do about the <problem>?
- Can you tell me?
- Do you know?
- How does that compare to industry average or known competition?
- Is this what you are striving for?

COACHING SKILL #26: PERIODICALLY ASSESS PROGRESS FROM COACHING

Attempt to get short-term, as well as longer-term assessments about benefits to justify your time commitments. Conclude each meeting by asking, "What are your top two takeaways from the session?", "What did you learn?' or 'How will you apply it?"

Gauge your employee's level of satisfaction and results from your coaching over longer periods of time by asking, "Where are you now versus when we started?" or "What does it mean to you?", "How does it feel?" or "How are you growing?' Ask the employee to identify the areas of need that have not yet been addressed and discuss how you can help to address those needs.

Not all your efforts will have the desired positive impact. You may decide to withdraw from the role because the time investment doesn't justify the effort. You may find a particular employee to be too stubborn to help with advice. You may find some employees won't take action. But for most of your employees, the results from your coaching will be good for the individual you coach and your organization.

COACHING EXAMPLE

Employee: I need to increase my sales performance.

Coach: What are some ways you could boost your performance?

Employee: I need to (a) update my scripts; and (b) make 10 more prospecting calls per week.

Coach: Excellent. When can you begin the script and implement making those calls?

Employee: Monday, right after the weekend.

Coach: Are you prepared to commit *fully* to what you have just said?

Employee: I'm going to go for it!

Coach: I'll note that as a commitment and bring it up as a follow-up item at our next review meeting.

COACHING ROLE WRAP UP

How much coaching are you doing? Just when you see the opportunity? How does this effort resonate with your employees? Do you see areas in which you should or could be coaching your employees, but are not? Do you see ways to be more effective with your coaching? How often do you find yourself giving advice or telling an employee what to do, when you should be interacting in a coaching role?

RATE YOURSELF

How far along do you think your coaching skill set is? Rate yourself on a scale of 1 to 10 as a coach. (1= I don't have a clue how to use this skill, 10 = I'm knocking it out of the park with this skill). Develop a strategy and plan for implementing coaching activities with selected employees whom you feel have the potential to make major contributions to your organization.

CONCLUSION

Mastering the coaching skills shared in this program will empower you to have the same high impact effect that High-Impact Managers have when coaching their employees.

HABIT 4

Creating a High-Performing Culture

Culture is the behavior that results when a group operates within a set of generally unspoken and unwritten rules. Organization Culture is the term given to the shared values and practices of your organization.

Your Organization Culture may be viewed as the environment that surrounds you at work, all of the time. It is made up of the values, beliefs, underlying assumptions, interests, experiences, and employees' behavior in the workplace. An Organization Culture tells people how to do their work. It takes its signals from leaders. It underlies work motivation, morale, creativity and success.

Some key points of an Organization's Culture should be put in writing. However, it is impossible to put in one written Organization Culture Statement all the values, beliefs, underlying assumptions, attitudes, and behaviors shared by a group of people.

Organization Culture shapes your work enjoyment, your work relationships, and your work processes. This culture is something you actually see through its manifestations by employees in your work place. In many ways, your Organization Culture is the personality of your organization expressed by employees through:

- Language
- Decision making
- Openness with other employees
- Stories and legends
- Daily work practices

BENEFITS OF A GREAT ORGANIZATION CULTURE

A good Organization Culture encourages everything and everyone in it to fulfill their desires around the tasks they complete for their jobs. This is a workplace with high morale and motivation—and thus high productivity. A good culture builds a more engaged and productive workplace, with a good balance between what we do with how we do it. It is a positive factor in bringing about greater impact by employees in the organization.

> To grow an organization to reach its maximum potential, High Impact Mangers need their subordinates to embrace the Organizational Culture.

A good Organization Culture is also a magnet for attracting good people to work for the organization.

THREE STEPS TO A HIGH IMPACT ORGANIZATION CULTURE

To achieve a High Impact Organization Culture, use the following three steps:

- Identify your current culture.
- Identify what you want the desired Organization Culture to be.
- Move everyone toward the desired culture.

STEP ONE: IDENTIFY YOUR CURRENT CULTURE

To change your culture, you need to see it for what it currently is. Your first step is to understand the culture that exists in your organization. Your assessment may or may not make you happy. Actually, your assessment may leave you very displeased. No matter what your culture assessment teaches, your culture is what it is.

HOW TO ASSESS YOUR CURRENT ORGANIZATIONAL CULTURE

It is difficult for many in management to objectively assess and understand their own Organization Culture. When people are at work on a daily basis, many of the manifestations of culture become almost invisible to them. To obtain an objective picture of your current Organizational Culture, consider the following:

- **Get feedback from your direct reports.** Meet as a group with those who report to you. Ask for their thoughts on what is good and what is bad about your current Organization Culture. Since it is difficult for many people to put into words what the culture is like, questions asked by you of your Direct Reports spark recognition of certain things that are happening or not happening.
- **Be an impartial observer of your culture in action.** Although it is hard to do, try with the eye of an outsider

to observe a group that you have never seen before. How do employees act? What do they do? Look for common behaviors and visible symbols. Watch for emotions. Emotions are indications of values. People do not get excited or upset about things that are unimportant to them. Examine conflicts closely for the same reason. How much emotion is expressed during the interaction?

- **Listen to your suppliers and your customers/ clients.** Consider comments expressed to you by those who interact with your organization. Look at what is written, in print and online, for information about what your Organization Culture really is.

- **Walk around the space occupied by your organization and look at physical signs of culture.** What is being communicated in the common areas of your organization's office, such as bulletin boards and objects that sit on desks or hang on walls? What is displayed on lockers or closets? Something as simple as your organization's bulletin board content and newsletters give clues as to your Organization Culture.

- **Consider what your employees are not discussing.** If nobody is discussing something that you think is important, this also helps you understand your Organization Culture.

- **How do employees communicate at work among themselves?** What do employees write to one another? What is said in memos or email? What is the tone of messages (formal or informal, pleasant or hostile, etc.)? How often do people communicate with one another? Is all communication written, or do people communicate verbally?

- **Interview employees in small groups.** Interview your employees in small groups and ask them to describe the Organization Culture. During these interviews, observe the behaviors and interaction patterns of employees in each group, in addition to hearing what they say about the culture. The following are examples of questions you can ask during a culture interview:

  ◊ What would you tell a friend about your organization, if he or she was considering working here?

  ◊ What one thing would you most like to change about this organization?

  ◊ Who is a hero around here? Why?

  ◊ What is your favorite characteristic present in our organization?

  ◊ What kinds of people fail in our organization?

  ◊ What would you recommend as a question to ask all candidates looking for jobs in our organization?

- **Conduct written culture surveys.** Written surveys taken by employees can provide insightful information about the Organization Culture. Those taking the survey must feel confident you will not share answers attributable to them. You can either purchase a standard survey from the web or custom-design a survey. A standard, non-customized survey should have interesting questions used in a number of other organizations. But it will not have customized questions especially relevant to your organization. The results of your survey will help provide clarity on your current Organizational Culture.

YOUR ORGANIZATION CULTURE IS NOT STAGNANT

Organization Culture will change with or without your direction. It either moves to your desired direction or on its own. As employees leave and replacements are hired, the culture may change. If there is a strong team culture, it may not change much. However, since each new employee brings their own values and practices to the group, the culture will change, at least a little. Even if personnel stay the same, the culture is likely to change. Of course, as subordinates age and the dynamics of their lives change, as they inevitably will, you may find the way they interact and their values at work also change.

The life cycle stage of the organization is also a factor. As it matures from a startup to a more established organization, the Organization Culture will change. But many other environmental factors impact the culture. As the environment in which the organization operates changes, the Organization Culture will also change.

> It's not unusual to find out that the actual culture in your organization does not match the *desired* culture of an organization.

These changes, major or minor, may be positive or they may not. The changes may be intended, but often they are not. The Organization Culture will change with or without your direction, so it is important you direct the changes when possible.

Once, at a luncheon with several business owners, I asked them to tell me one thing they didn't like about their Organization Culture. Here are some of the responses:

- Feel threatened by change
- Negativity
- Unable to admit being wrong
- The blame game
- Credit hogs
- Failure to be accountable for following established processes and systems
- Not replacing employees who refuse to embrace new culture
- Not qualifying new hires based upon culture fit
- Managers who are part of the culture problem

Later, I will talk about ways to neutralize these negative culture factors.

STEP TWO: IDENTIFY WHAT THE DESIRED ORGANIZATION CULTURE SHOULD BE

Before you can change it, you must decide what you want the Organization Culture to look like in the future. Different organizations—whether profit, non-profit or government departments—should have different cultures that fit the desires of those who are key decision makers.

Identify cultural elements that support the success of your organization.

What are the kinds of values, habits and basic beliefs that your employees need to share to support your organization's vision or mission? Your employees may be different in many ways; but for the team to work effectively, there must be shared core values and beliefs.

Once you know the Organization Culture you are designing is what you want to have, express it in a "Written Culture

Statement." It's not possible for your Written Culture Statement to include all the things you want to see in the Organization Culture, but you should identify the most important thing.

The following are examples of Written Culture Statements from three different organizations:

FIRST ORGANIZATION'S WRITTEN CULTURE STATEMENT

- Our employees will contribute to and embrace change. Creative thinking leading to change is an important part of our culture. Employees will welcome, initiate, feel empowered by and engaged by change this is essential to compete in today's quickly changing marketplace.
- Employees will receive recognition for their accomplishments. Every employee should receive the recognition they deserve for the things they brought about.
- No employee will bring negative energy to the organization. Employees must accept and embrace the importance of positive energy. We will avoid negative attack-style interactions and foster an atmosphere that encourages creativity and out-of-the-box ideas.
- We are open to employees' ideas and suggestions. Challenging comments to what we do or don't do are to be expected and appreciated, rather than an indication someone is not a "team player." If leaders show they are open to ideas and suggestions, employees and managers will quickly join them.
- We will share information within the organization so we can operate at the most effective and creative levels. We will share information that goes beyond what employees need to just do their job. Information that

doesn't seem relevant to their jobs at the moment may help them connect with ideas of great value.

- We will focus on what can be done, even though we may not always succeed. We will not avoid decisions or take the easy way out because of a fear of failing. Mistakes will be made. However, if these mistakes take place within the cultural values we desire, we will learn from them and use this knowledge to bring about greater success for the organization.

SECOND ORGANIZATION'S WRITTEN CULTURE STATEMENT

We will have a culture where:

- No employee fears expressing views, including the right to question decisions and priorities. Their views will be heard.
- All employees will give their total support when decisions are made, even if decisions aren't in accord with their views, so that we speak with one voice.
- All management will model the cultural behavior we ask of our employees.
- Management will "walk the talk" with actions, not just words.
- Employees will do the right thing when dealing with other employees, resources and customers.
- Employees will be ambassadors for the organization at all times with all possible audiences.
- Disputes and disagreements must be handled internally with only the appropriate people involved.
- Work hard, but have fun and celebrate success.

- Be open to change and doing things differently.
- Don't stop doing what works because of ego or any other reason.
- Give customers the benefit of the doubt, although the customer is not always right.

THIRD ORGANIZATION'S WRITTEN CULTURE STATEMENT

Our employees will:

- Display to the best of their ability, on a day-in, day-out basis, the core values of honesty, teamwork, respect, accountability and passion.
- Be accountable for staying committed to deadlines/timelines.
- Deliver, in its final form, a work product that is top quality.
- Give no excuses for not keeping commitments or producing inferior work.
- Proactively communicate to those to whom you have given deadline commitments if you fall behind the deadline.
- Communicate with employees with openness and respect.
- Do not misrepresent yourself or deceive other employees.
- Prepare for scheduled meetings.
- Refuse to participate in gossip and don't tolerate gossip at work when it takes place.
- Communicate in a professional manner to all clients at all times.
- Proactively think, "Who else needs to know what I'm doing, or what just happened?"

Now is the time to identify the culture you want for your organization. Look at the examples above for things you want for your culture, but don't limit yourself just to these examples.

STEP THREE: MOVE EVERYONE TOWARD THE DESIRED CULTURE

Now it is time to start reshaping your Organization Culture. You have a Written Organization Culture Statement for the environment, but this statement is meaningless unless you gain buy-in to your desired culture through actions, not words. You make this culture happen through your actions and your responses to activities that are inconsistent with the expectations of the organization.

In some cases, you will need to focus on easy-to-implement changes. On the other hand, if much change is needed, you may need to create a formal plan to ensure that the desired Organization Culture becomes a reality.

CHANGING THE CULTURE TO WHAT YOU WANT TAKES TIME

The typical managerial nature is to cut to the chase and make things happen quickly. However, taking the indirect—and sometimes less time-intensive— route to change is sometimes the most effective way to get the desired results.

Also, the size of your organization will impact how fast the cultural changes are embraced. Change in small companies comes faster than in big ones because fewer employees need to see the light.

My first experience with changing culture involved a company that was in legal receivership. The timeline for changing the culture was much slower than I had hoped for.

There was a high level of entrenchment on the part of some employees to the culture they had worked in for years. (If employees are deeply entrenched in a culture that you do not want, it may be best to move slowly or wait. Organization Cultures develop with an evolutionary process rather than overnight.)

Some changes I wanted began almost overnight. Still, it was at least a year before the bulk of the new culture was solidly in place. It is more difficult to change an existing culture than to create a culture in a brand-new organization. When an organization has been around for a long time, people must unlearn old values, assumptions, and behaviors, before they can learn new ones.

IT TAKES A COMMITMENT TO CHANGE CULTURE

The degree to which you commit to make culture change happen, as well as the level of execution and follow-through, will affect the time needed to change your Organization Culture and even whether the change ever takes place.

SUPPORT FROM YOUR DIRECT REPORTS

Bringing about the Organization Culture you want requires a commitment from you and your direct reports. Even though you set the desired culture, ultimately it's your direct reports who are responsible for making it happen with the employees who report to them. You and those who report to you must commit to "walk the talk," instead of just "talking the talk."

Hold a meeting with those who report directly to you to jump-start the culture change process. Discuss the values you want them to embrace. Encourage their feedback about the culture. Let them know of your level of commitment to the change and the actions you will take to demonstrate that behavior inconsistent with the culture will not be ignored.

Get commitments from your direct reports on how each of them will involve lower-level employees to build the powerful and productive workplace culture you desire.

COMMUNICATIONS TO BRING ABOUT CULTURE CHANGE

First, determine which employees in the organization are "spheres of influence" whose buy-in is critical to making your culture change happen. Set up private meetings with them to discuss what you are trying to accomplish and why. Share what you think will be the positive impact of culture change on each employee's job.

Your next step is to share the written Culture Statement with employees, using all channels of communication at all levels. Some meetings will be with groups of your employees, such as the warehouse staff. When employees meet together, each sees where others in their group fit, and this helps develop group culture.

Determine what is the maximum group size in which want to communicate as a group. Choose a location for each of your group culture meetings. Determine the schedule for your culture change meetings and stick to it. Determine who will be the best one to lead communications about culture at these meetings. It may or may not be you.

Follow a written agenda to keep these meetings on target and prevent them from going off on tangents. Explain each point in the written Culture Statement. Follow this with a statement of benefits that comes about from the desired culture and conclude with a clear message of culture accountability expectations.

> Your employees need to understand that you do not view your Written Organization Culture Statement as just lip-service.

It is essential that you maintain control of your emotions at these meetings and that you use active listening techniques so as to avoid communication miscues. Focus on *really* hearing and understanding the meaning of what is being said.

After the meetings have taken place, follow up with some form of written communications to all employees.

AFTER CULTURE COMMUNICATIONS MEETINGS HAVE TAKEN PLACE

You and those who report directly to you should announce rewards for actions that are in alignment with the desired Organization Culture (and also describe consequences when actions are out of alignment.) Employees learn to perform certain behaviors through rewards or through negative consequences. When a behavior gets rewarded, it is repeated and the association eventually becomes part of the culture.

Identify ways your reward system can be changed to encourage the desired Organization Culture behaviors. This includes financial rewards and recognition rewards. A simple "Thank you," for work performed in a particular manner, for example, can help mold the culture. A promotion denied for lack of the right values or attitude will also convey a message.

COMMON CULTURE ROADBLOCKS

High-Impact Managers face roadblocks to creating the culture they want, but they are proactive in developing and using tactics for getting around them. Here are common roadblocks that can keep your plans from succeeding and suggestions for dealing with them.

> **High-Impact Managers create culture with their actions, not their words.**

CULTURAL ROADBLOCK #1: FEEL THREATENED BY CHANGE

Those who feel threatened by change are not likely to embrace changes in the organization's culture. They will question the direction of change and share their resistance with others. If left unchecked, this can lead to smoldering hostility. These employees will become obstacles to the success of cultural change.

One way to address this behavior is by proactively resolving the conflict. Schedule time to meet with a resistant employee in order to address and resolve his issues. Give your full effort towards achieving buy-in for cultural change.

CULTURAL ROADBLOCK #2: NEGATIVITY

One of the most common cultural challenges is changing a negative mindset or negativity throughout the organization. A negative work environment is likely to result in employees who are emotionally exhausted, irritable and anxious. This, in turn, leads to underperformance and employee turnover.

Implement whatever actions are needed to neutralize

negativity among employees. This will go a long way towards removing negativity from the workplace.

In one case, a manager had to address an outspoken employee who never had a good thing to say about anything. The manager met with the employee to discuss her negative attitude and let her know that it had to stop. Instead of accepting or acknowledging her negative attitude, the employee stated that her coworkers didn't appreciate her, didn't do their fair share of work and spent too much time on personal matters. The manager asked her to be more specific with her complaints and then made clear that if she had anything negative to express, she should speak to him directly. He told her the organization could not tolerate her creating a negative atmosphere for her fellow employees.

CULTURAL ROADBLOCK #3: UNABLE TO ADMIT BEING WRONG

Many organizations have a cultural pattern of employees not admitting their mistakes because they think such an admission will rob them of other employees' respect. Let your employees know that others will respect them more, and emulate their example, when they readily admit their mistakes and move forward.

One organization spent over $800,000 developing a new computer software program that was not operating effectively. The organization continued to pour money into improving the product. Every manager (except the CIO who had conceived of the idea for the software program) could see that it was never going to work right, but had become a "sacred cow." The CEO should have seen that the CIO's inability to admit his mistake and develop a course change would encourage similar behavior among others in the organization. But resources were wasted on the software program long after it should have been discontinued. This showed other employees an incorrect example of not being willing to admit mistakes and adjust as needed to counteract those mistakes.

By contrast, look at how the owner of a food-production organization handled a similar problem. The owner had created a new cookie product that was losing a large sum of money. Despite this fact, another organization with greater distribution capabilities had expressed an interest in buying the product.

Several of the organization's executives recommended selling off the assets of the new cookie product. The owner of the organization admitted his mistake and approved the sale. He did not allow the cookie product, which had also been his "baby," to become a sacred cow. The sale of the product eliminated large losses and provided valuable proceeds used to promote other exciting new products. Admitting his mistake and making the right follow-up decisions eliminated a potential roadblock to a needed course change.

We all make mistakes. How these mistakes are acknowledged and handled is a major factor that separates organizations with high achievement from those that never reach a level of success. An organization is more effective when employees admit they are wrong (appropriately) and move on to correct the problem. This two-word phrase – "I'm wrong" – is one of the most difficult things for some people to say, yet a culture in which employees admit when they are wrong can often work wonders. (The same principle applies to the CEO and members of his or her executive team.)

CULTURAL ROADBLOCK #4–THE BLAME GAME

There's no place in a high impact organization culture for the "blame game." This is a pattern of shifting blame for anything that goes wrong to someone else. Playing the blame game brings about a culture in which decisions are made based upon what has the least amount of risk, rather than what has the greatest potential for high impact change. It also results in actions not being taken that should be taken, due to fear of being blamed if actions don't succeed. The blame game culture leaves employees stressful and emotionally exhausted.

If your employees play the blame game, it's likely their subordinates will avoid taking actions with a high level of risk and reward. The employee of one company told me he based decisions on taking no risks, because he had learned the key to working for his boss was to "cover your ass." He explained that his boss made sure all the blame went to his fellow subordinates when anything went wrong. It's easy to see how a culture that allows the blame game cannot operate at its peak efficiency.

CULTURAL ROADBLOCK #5–CREDIT HOGS

If you want a culture in which employees work towards the greatest productivity, you must be committed to showing appreciation and giving credit to the person who deserves the credit.

Credit hogs create a disincentive to make the extra effort in doing things for the organization. Try to determine what causes the credit hog to act the way he or she does. For example, does the credit hog see others who deserve credit as a threat?

Credit hogs create a disincentive to take the extra step or make the extra effort in doing things for the organization. Try to figure out what is causing the credit hog to act the way he or she is acting. For example, is the credit hog acting as he does because he sees the person who deserves the credit as a threat? Meet with the credit hog and ask flat out why he or she takes credit for others work.

CULTURAL ROADBLOCK #6 – FAILURE TO BE ACCOUNTABLE FOR FOLLOWING ESTABLISHED PROCESSES AND SYSTEMS

Tolerating poor performance or a failure to hold people accountable for not following established processes and systems will impede your organization's success. Addressing this issue may be difficult, but failing to do so is irresponsible. Mentally prepare yourself for actions you need to in order to overcome this cultural challenge.

CULTURAL ROADBLOCK #7 – NOT REPLACING EMPLOYEES WHO REFUSE TO EMBRACE NEW CULTURE

Give employees who do not immediately embrace your desired culture a reasonable amount of time to fit in. If nothing you say or do works to change their behavior, you may need to replace them with new employees who fit your culture.

CULTURAL ROADBLOCK #8 –NOT QUALIFYING NEW HIRES BASED UPON CULTURE FIT

When a prospective employee interviews for a job in your organization, make it a top priority to determine whether they are a good cultural fit. During the interview process, ask the applicant if he or she sees himself or herself as a good fit with your culture.

You can form an initial opinion about the applicant early in the interview process, though you can never know for sure. Still, there's a high likelihood you will know when you have found the right candidate.

CULTURE ROADBLOCK #9–SUBCULTURES

Employees learn subculture behaviors by interacting with fellow employees and receiving some type of psychic reward from them. (For example, employees may make fun of a manager behind her back.) These subculture behaviors are out of line with most desired Organization Cultures.

If you are aware of a negative subculture, proactively address it with all employees involved.

CULTURE ROADBLOCK #10–MANAGERS WHO ARE PART OF THE CULTURE PROBLEM

Your management must lead culture change by changing their behavior. Tell them what is expected of them in order to make Organization Culture happen.

HABIT 5

Retain Your Best Employees

When you lose a good long-term employee, it takes time and money to recruit and hire replacement employees. Replacing the employee distracts from efforts that could be made for making the organization more successful, rather than spending time recruiting, hiring and training replacements.

When an experienced employee leaves your organization, you lose all of their accumulated institutional knowledge. Higher impact results are more likely to take place when your best employees have been with the organization for many years. Institutional knowledge leads to greater contributions to your organization's results. By contrast, new employees take time to learn their jobs and the history of factors involved in doing their jobs right.

Because of all of the above, retaining your best employees should be among your most important management responsibilities.

My objective in creating this program is to help you to identify the reasons why your best employees may leave and show you how to develop proactive retention strategies to eliminate these reasons. Developing your retention strategies will be easier to do once you understand the strategies used by High-Impact Managers to keep their best employees.

STRATEGY 1: COMPENSATE COMPETITIVELY

Even your best employees may be inclined to leave your organization if they feel they are being significantly underpaid. Offering competitive wages alone will not solve problems in retaining your best employees. But paying competitive wages with competitive benefits will eliminate one of the primary reasons employees decide to go elsewhere.

PERFORMANCE-BASED COMPENSATION PLANS

Provide incentive compensation programs that give financial rewards for outstanding work results. These incentive plans, sometimes referred to as "results-based compensation programs," bring about greater employee engagement in achieving high-level performance. Performance-based incentives motivate employees to achieve at a higher level and encourage them to stay with an organization. Incentive plans are not possible for all jobs but, with creativity, you can introduce some level of performance compensation for most positions.

A completion bonus is a one form of performance-based compensation that is effective for individuals in positions with high objectives and clear measurements. Prizes can be more motivating for some employees than cash rewards or bonuses.

Some incentives involve relatively low-cost prizes, such as tickets to a sporting event. Other prizes may be much more expensive. For example, one organization offers a trip each year to the employee with the best annual sales result and also rewards a trip to the sales manager at a store with the least number of customer complaints.

STAY INFORMED

Stay informed of the current compensation ranges in your area. Try to pinpoint industry-specific salary levels. The conditions of a particular industry often result in pay levels significantly different from those for comparable positions in other industries. Knowledge of industry standards of pay rates and benefits will help determine strategies for retaining your key employees.

Recently, the CFO in an organization complained about an accountant who quit his organization after 15 years of employment. After being advised to check on whether she had been paid in a competitive manner, the CFO found that the compensation was, in fact, *not* competitive. The position she accepted with another organization came with a much higher salary. The CFO realized he needed to pay a higher salary to get someone with his former employee's skills, due to the competitive market for those experienced in this line of work.

INFORMATION FROM GOVERNMENT AGENCIES

In most countries, states and provinces, government agencies issue, via the internet, wage survey information, which show wages paid in local job markets for many jobs, ranging from office workers and technical positions to top-level management and executive positions. This information typically classifies jobs according to skill and responsibility levels. For example, ten different levels for administrative assistants: One level might be for those who work for the heads of large organizations and are assumed to have broad responsibilities. Another level might be for those who work for lower-level supervisors and have the least responsibilities of any administrative assistant classification.

INFORMATION FROM YOUR PARTICULAR INDUSTRY

One way to get information about competitive salaries for your industry is to check for data released by a professional or trade association. There is an association for almost every imaginable profession or trade and most perform salary surveys. Be cautious with results from association surveys if they rely heavily upon data received from large organization employers. These employers are likely to pay more than the average pay of smaller organizations in your industry.

Find data that classifies wage levels by the size of the organization employer in your type of industry. Compare your employees' total compensation program against those with similar responsibilities and functions employed by organizations of similar size to your own. Then rank positions in terms of scope of responsibility and decision-making authority.

If your compensation package is competitive, share this information with your employees. While people may still complain about money, they will at least see their salaries are equitable. You may have to point out that small and mid-size organizations generally pay less than larger organizations for quality personnel, but there are advantages in working at a company like yours (such as being able to know the owners of the organization).

EMPLOYEE BENEFITS

To determine whether your compensation is competitive, consider employee benefits in addition to salary or hourly compensation. To be competitive, you need to offer your employees the best benefits package you can afford. However, always keep in mind that such benefits can greatly affect the true cost of employee compensation.

Take time to learn your industry's fringe benefits, incentive plans and other forms of non-salary or hourly compensation with organizations of your size and financial situation. Then determine what benefits you can afford to provide.

Online resources in almost every country can help develop customized benefits websites for employers. These "self-service benefit centers" give employees direct, detailed access to information about the organization's benefits programs and also provides links to benefits providers. Some benefit centers also provide access to information such as organization newsletters.

Does your organization provide unusual benefits not offered by similar organizations? For example, some organizations provide employee loans under certain conditions (along with specific limits and terms for repayment). If you decide to create this benefit, determine a policy for which you can provide employee loans. Put the policy in writing, so employees will understand if and why they are turned down for a loan.

One option is to establish an "employee loan fund" with a predetermined amount of money set aside for loans. The loans are provided to employees under strict rules and terms, including a limit on the amount of any loan to any one employee. (For example, a loan might be for no more than the employee's net wages for one workweek.) The payment schedule established for the fund might call for repayment of $50 per week with no missed repayments or "skips," allowed. Generally, these loans are repaid by authorized and automatic payroll deduction.

Continually communicate, explain and sell the value of the benefits you provide to employees. Quantify how much employee benefits cost your organization. Selling the value of your benefits sounds obvious, but it isn't always so. Most organizations do a terrible job of it.

PUT COMPENSATION PROGRAM IN WRITING

After you have discussed compensation, bonuses, incentives, etc., prepare a memo that summarizes compensation and other rewards, with all conditions relating to them clearly set forth in the memo. Not putting the program in writing can lead to employees having different ideas of what they believe you said. Then they will have no trust in what you say in the future and will be more likely to look for other employment.

PAY STRUCTURE NEEDED FOR HOURLY EMPLOYEES WHO DO THE SAME JOB

If your organization has several hourly employees doing the same type of work, one way to reduce hourly-level employees from quitting your organization is to post hourly wage ranges or grids by work classifications. This published information should show which positions fall within what ranges, categorized by such factors as skills and the number of years an employee has been with the organization. There needs to be a base wage for each category. There must also be a pay increase element based upon how long an employee has been with the organization. This results in hourly employees feeling they are being treated in an equal way. It also lets hourly employees know what is needed to move to the current top of the wage range, based upon their job classification.

STRATEGY 2: MAKE RECOGNITION PART OF YOUR ORGANIZATION'S DNA

Recognition is an important emotional reward that increases employee motivation and engagement, which, in turn, increases the likelihood of recognized employees staying with your organization. Employees who receive public recognition are more likely to feel connected to your organization. They will also want to achieve their top performance level and make their highest impact at work. Providing recognition minimizes their focus on issues that may adversely affect the way they feel.

> **Lack of employee recognition contributes to poor retention.**

You can guide your employees to greater longevity with your organization through such recognition efforts. High-Impact Managers take the time to look for ways to demonstrate appreciation by giving recognition.

DEVELOP A RECOGNITION PLAN

High-Impact Managers typically plan both private and public employee recognition. Be creative in showing public recognition. Periodically change up what you do in order to retain your best people.

Here are common ways (and some more creative ways) to show public recognition.

PUBLIC RECOGNITION

Recognize employees who have attained milestones, such as work anniversaries or birthday parties. Do you have a monthly newsletter? If so, recognizing milestones like birthdays and work achievements should be a big section in every month's issue.

One of the most common ways to give public recognition is by recognizing employees who have attained milestones, such as birthday parties. Buying a cake and taking a small amount of time for all employees to celebrate those who have had birthdays during each month is a common practice. Do you have a monthly newsletter? If so, recognizing milestones such as birthdays, as well as achievements should be one section in every month's newsletter.

> **Create and periodically review your strategies for employee recognition.**

Public acknowledgement and celebrations should also take place for employees who attain work longevity or milestones of years employed with your organization. Include plaques or trophies for those who have been there a key number of years, or for those who have achieved something special. It might surprise you to know how many employees proudly display a plaque or trophy in their home. During a visit to an employee's home, I saw three recognition trophies on the fireplace mantel (lighting had been created to shine on these trophies). Plaques and trophies are symbols of recognition that go far beyond the moment of celebration.

Many organizations give employees public recognition for a job well done at an annual organization event. Schedule annual meetings with all or groups of employees during which such achievements are recognized. Share appropriate performance results data for awards that are based upon measurable results.

> **During annual meetings, spend the time needed to recognize employee who have achieved milestones.**

Most awards given at annual organization events will be for measurable results. But some can mark special efforts in helping employees or customers and for suggestions resulting in dramatic changes or innovations. One organization annually honors five employees who did the most during the calendar year to reinforce the organization's values.

These publicly given annual awards, based on non-measurable results, also mean a lot to those who are recognized. Employees appreciate their fellow employees becoming aware that they have provided something special to the organization.

CREATIVE WAYS TO SHOW PUBLIC RECOGNITION

Let me share a couple of cost-effective ways used to creatively recognize employees. One organization bought two toys—a "strongman toy," given each month to the employee who helped keep the team strong, and a "care bear," given each month to an employee who went above and beyond in a caring way to help other employees.

Another organization developed a preprinted postcard that any employee could use to recognize another employee for an effort above and beyond the norm. Any employee can decide at any time if, when, who and why to give the award. This creative,

> **If you wait to give recognition, you may be too late to keep your employee.**

but very simple, recognition award helps increase the ties that both the person giving and the person receiving the award have with the organization.

PRIVATE RECOGNITION

There is a saying, "Praise in public and admonish in private." Praising in private also has great value. When you meet privately with your subordinates, commend something the individual has done well. Also, don't wait for a scheduled meeting to pass on any positive comments about the employee made by others.

STRATEGY 3: HAVE EMPLOYEE DEVELOPMENT ASSISTANCE PROGRAMS

One of the most powerful things you can do is to pay for additional employee training. Upgrading his or her skill sets through outside training programs helps an employee learn skills that will improve his or her performance and may help move the employee into positions that keep the employee with your organization.

Organizations with great retention typically make employee development a key part of the organization's DNA. There are many ways organizations can encourage or even sponsor a philosophy of continuous lifelong learning. Developmental sponsoring typically involves the organization making an investment in the development of the individual employee.

Not all employees are interested in personal development. Some will accept developmental guidance and others will set up personal barriers with excuses of why they will not do what they could for developmental growth. However, the type of employee whom you don't want to lose is typically someone who takes well to developmental opportunities that also help improve the performance of the organization. In some positions, a lack of desire or response to development opportunities may mean these employees are not the right people for their positions.

Developmental guidance is usually best done in private, identifying potential tools for achieving success. One common tool involves a formal tuition assistance program. Organizations with such programs generally establish a maximum budget to be allocated for a year, with a formula and guidelines for helping employees pay for classes, certificates and degrees—for example, paying for an employee to learn as software program that will help him or her become more proficient at their job.

> **Train your management to seek out learning opportunities for their subordinates and the employees who report to their subordinates.**

Most organizations pay for employee classes that they view as likely to bring about a good return on their investment. They contribute only to courses they consider to be career related. They typically define career related topics more loosely with executive level employees than they do with others. These organizations also have minimum definitions of academic success needed to qualify for contributions. It is common to find that they will only reimburse employees if they obtain a B average or greater in a course.

Many organizations require employees to repay costs for

outside training if the employee quits his or her job within a specified period of time, such as one year from the completion date of training. Some organizations will pay for half of the tuition at the time employees sign up for the classes and pay the other half when the employees prove they have attained a designated minimum grade-point average. Other organizations pay none of the initial tuition, but will reimburse the full tuition for classes they have approved in advance and for which the employee receives a minimum grade that the organization designates as "academic success."

> **Allocate training for your best employees in every way you can justify in your budget.**

Look beyond the current skills and experience of the employees. Think about the potential they have for learning new skills and the behavioral characteristics that will make them do so. Consider which employees will develop into higher impact employees who can achieve success in future job openings in the organization.

STRATEGY 4: WORK ENVIRONMENT EMPLOYEES WANT TO BE PART OF

In many team sports, players say they gave that extra winning effort because they were playing for someone (or something) "beyond themselves." In a similar manner, many of your best employees like to feel part of—and to contribute to—something bigger than them.

Bringing about a positive work atmosphere does not happen by accident. When you make your workplace atmosphere as enjoyable as possible, your employees are less likely to look elsewhere for employment.

The right type of workplace environment drives the kind of success you want in the long term. Here are some ways you can create this work environment.

RESPECT

Many employees quit jobs because they believe they are not being treated with respect. Consistently show your employees respect on a daily basis and they will be much less likely to look for work somewhere else. They will give the extra effort needed to help bring about a work atmosphere that others want to experience.

Some acts of disrespect are subtle, such as when you pay attention to your smartphone or computer while speaking to an employee or meeting with them in their weekly one-on-one reviews. Other forms of disrespect, such as yelling at an employee, are anything but subtle.

> **A manager yelling at an employee will undo many good things.**

CALLING EACH OTHER BY FIRST NAMES

Most employees prefer a work atmosphere in which they feel comfortable using the first names of their co-workers, including those at higher levels in the organization. You can form a stronger psychological connection when you call your employees by their first names.

FLEXIBILITY

Strive to accommodate flexible work hours when possible, if and when personal emergencies occur. Allow flexible dress codes if this does not detrimentally impact the image you want with customers or clients. (Of course, you need to adapt as needed; you might not want to meet potential investors in jeans or short skirts.)

OWNERSHIP OF THEIR JOBS

Give your employees a sense of ownership of their jobs by providing the authority needed to get the job done without you micromanaging every detail. Responsibility without authority creates a frustrating workplace.

Your best employees value an environment in which they have clear responsibility, along with the tools needed to do the job. This includes allowing employees to offer input and suggestions on refining or creating new workplace processes.

This input will take place where there is an open management style with open lines of communication. Make your style as open as it can be without hurting efficiency. When employees can make a difference, they feel that what they do is important to the bigger picture—and it is.

> In an open, two-way communication workplace atmosphere, be prepared to respond honestly without sounding defensive or dismissive.

When you receive input, respond with real-time feedback or your employee will feel he or she is not being heard. Draw out ideas. Engage in genuine two-way dialogue in which employees communicate their ideas about things that both excite and concern them.

APPLY POLICIES IN A CONSISTENT WAY

Another situation that can take the fun out of the workplace atmosphere is when policies are applied inconsistently. This happens when one or more employees get special treatment. This will upset other employ-

> **When you apply policies consistently, you eliminate feelings about double standards.**

ees and make them think about leaving the organization. Consistent application of policies, therefore, is a must if you expect to retain your best employees.

At some point, every manager has faced a situation that requires him or her to consider allowing an employee not follow a particular policy. Such situations are simply unavoidable, but don't lose sight of the fact that this treatment will impact workplace morale. Special treatment relating to the inconsistent enforcement of policies leads to dissatisfied employees who may ultimately quit. If you feel an exception must be made, make sure it is a highly unusual circumstance.

Sometimes the problem is caused by some managers enforcing a policy, while other managers do not. For example, an executive allowed one employee in his department to work from home one day a week, but did not offer the same arrangement to others. An upcoming star, whose manager turned down her request to work one day per week at home, was so upset that she took another job.

REWARD TEAM PERFORMANCE

People like to feel part of a team. One way of creating an atmosphere with employee team connection is by rewarding team

> **Inconsistent employee policy enforcement leads to employee discontent and often causes top performers to leave.**

performance, instead of just rewarding an individual.

This can be done with team completion bonuses, prizes or other incentives to recognize what an employee team achieves.

The reward doesn't have to be financial. After a tough project, giving all responsible team members some time off is typically much appreciated. For example, after employees at one restaurant volunteered to do extra work on a particular weekend, each were given orchestra seat tickets to a musical appearing locally and the time off to attend. Later, the employees could not stop talking about their night out and how they felt so appreciated.

By rewarding a team of employees, you create peer pressure for each person not to let other team members down. Under this approach, fellow team members encourage each other to commit to team results.

EMPLOYEE SOCIAL EVENTS

Social events paid for by the organization help build a friendly workplace. After-hour employee group activities or socialization strengthen loyalty and improve job satisfaction. Enjoying periodic meals together or attending a musical or sporting event also fosters valuable bonding.

ALL WORKING TOWARDS THE SAME VISION FOR THE ORGANIZATION'S FUTURE

Employees need to understand and believe in the vision for the organization's long-term future. They want to see how they fit into this vision as well.

ALIGNMENT AMONG MANAGEMENT

Employees don't like a workplace atmosphere in which they feel caught between conflicting views of managers. Employees are more likely to stay with organizations where everyone is "on the same page."

> **Check out *AlignUp* for an online management development program I developed that will help your organization bring about an aligned workplace. I also recommend that you read my book, *The Aligned Workplace*.**

Lack of alignment within an organization is often the source of employee dissatisfaction. For example, a capable employee who had quickly moved up the ladder in an organization eventually quit because he was tired of managers working at cross-purposes with one another. The lack of alignment in the organization brought about an atmosphere that was frustrating to the employee.

STRATEGY 5: IDENTIFY CAREER PATHS FOR EMPLOYEES WITH POTENTIAL TO GROW

Identifying opportunities for future promotions is an important way to retain your best employees. They need to feel there are promotions in their future, based upon objective standards of doing outstanding work, along with maintaining certain attitudes that fit the job to which they hope to be promoted.

Your best employees also need to know where they stand with you. They want to have an opportunity to move into roles that make greater use of their strengths and come with more responsibilities and higher income potential. If they don't see this, they may look elsewhere for these opportunities.

For employees to see their career paths, it is important that you discuss possible career paths or advancement opportunities that you see for your subordinates and then find out if these are the career paths that they would like to follow.

To the extent that you can discuss it, share information about future position openings and the job descriptions for these possible openings. Also share some level of information about the timing of the projected openings.

PROMOTING FROM WITHIN

If you have the talent in your organization, it is wise to promote from within when a higher paying job opens up and replace the promoted person by promoting someone else in your organization, and so on. Promoting from within is a great employee motivator, contributing to morale and increasing the likelihood of employees staying with your organization.

Another benefit of promoting from within means you will not have to deal with the unknowns of bringing someone in from outside your organization. Your employees has demonstrated high capability in her current position, has a positive attitude, a good work ethic, etc. The employee promoted from within also has needed knowledge about your organization's people, products and services. All these factors give that person a higher probability for success in the position.

Identify employees in your organization who deserve to be considered for a promotion. Recognize that when you fill new openings with current employees, you may need to include a plan to train up and develop the promoted employees to handle their new responsibilities.

PROMOTING AN EMPLOYEE TO A MANAGEMENT POSITION

When a management position opens up, consider which of the former manager's subordinates could be effective in the position. You will need to be cautious if the subordinate you are considering has not before held a management position.

> **Promote from within whenever possible.**

The promotion of a great IT employee or salesperson to a management position can be a mistake, because the skill set for being effective at managing is very different than what is needed for effectively "doing non-management work."

RIGHT FIT FOR WHO THEY ARE

If you can't create a path to get your best people to the positions where they are most likely to do well, they probably won't be happy at work. If they are not happy, they are more likely to find work somewhere else.

Getting employees into the right jobs should be based on their particular strengths. The more they move up, the more the positions should call for them to use their talents more effectively.

One of your challenges is to make sure that the career path you identify for an employee gives him or her the opportunity to do what they do best. Often, this will require you to find ways for these employees to develop these strengths and skills, so they are ready when these talents are needed in new positions as they move ahead in their careers.

BELIEF IN THE ORGANIZATION'S FUTURE

Having a long-term career path requires an employee to believe in the future of the organization. If an employee does not have this belief, he or she will likely go to another organization in which they have greater faith in the future.

For example, the owner of a successful service business shared how one of his best long-term executives had just given notice the day before. He said he was "blindsided" and had no idea the man was even considering leaving his employment. The executive told the owner that the decision was prompted by the company owner that his daughter was being groomed to take over as CEO. The executive said that while he liked the owner's daughter personally, he thought that she would run the organization "into the ground." He felt he needed to work at an organization where he could feel more confident about the future.

STRATEGY 6: CHANGE MINDS OF EMPLOYEES WHO WANT TO LEAVE

Sometimes you will hear one of your employees is looking for another job. At this point, it is useful to consider the following question: Do you want to retain the person? Only then can you decide what to do about it.

WHEN YOU DON'T WANT TO CHANGE THE MIND OF THE EMPLOYEE

It's not always bad when an employee leaves your organization. If you decide you don't want to change his mind, you will face the time-consuming tasks of recruiting, hiring, and training needed to replace him. Sometimes this can be a blessing in disguise. Your new employee might be better qualified to handle the position and may make a more positive impact on the organization than the employee who is leaving. In many cases, replacement employees turn out to be stars who take on more responsibilities than the former employees ever had.

Also, a resignation may force you to re-evaluate your organization's current personnel structure. All too often, when an employee leaves, it results in entirely eliminating the position and reorganizing responsibilities among other employees. Sometimes this results in making other long-overdue personnel changes that couldn't be made while the former employee was working for you.

Your employee may have reasons for quitting that negate any efforts on your part to retain her. For example, your organization may be better off without an employee who is "burned out." If this is the reason given by the employee for leaving, it may be best that you don't try to change her mind, since you're probably incurring costs due to the employee's inefficiency.

If the employee is quitting because he feels the job is no longer needed, you may want to retain him by "inventing" a position that can use the employee's skills in a different area. However, give serious thought to this because inventing positions that are not needed may result in just delaying the inevitable of losing the employee.

WHEN YOU WANT TO CHANGE THE MIND OF THE EMPLOYEE

If you decide to try to change the mind of the employee who has decided to leave your organization, find out why he wants to quit and try to overcome the reason or reasons. Say something like, "I would like to keep you with our organization and maybe I could change your mind if you share with me the reasons you want to leave."

Some of the best employees I've had over the years, had, at some point, given notice of their resignations. After I became aware of their intentions, we discussed why they wanted to leave. We then came up with a course of action resulting in many of them staying and turning out to be successful, long-term employees.

Let's look at some common reasons for leaving and how they might be handled to change the employee's mind.

OFFERED GREATER COMPENSATION

If an employee resigns because of an offer of greater compensation from another organization, consider whether you want to match or exceed the offer. Taking this action might have a negative impact on other employees. The ripple effect from a response to a competitive offer may be costly in both dollars and bruised egos, with other employees leaving your organization as a result.

WORKING WITH PEERS NOT CONDUCIVE TO WORK SATISFACTION

Organizations have problems retaining their best people if they have to work with others whom they feel are not conducive to sustained levels of work satisfaction. When some of your employees have an apathetic attitude, it results in lower efficiency, productivity, and innovation. This lack of employee engagement has a tendency to cause frustration among your best people, moving them to leave your organization because they don't want to be part of this group.

Your best employees will likely stay and grow with your organization if they see that you expect all employees to demonstrate values that are aligned with those of the organization. They want to work with other employees who want to help their organization succeed.

Your best people won't want to work for an organization that "looks the other way" at employees who constantly complain. If you ignore employees who are chronic complainers, you are inviting an atmosphere of bad morale that will cause an exodus of employees.

> If a direct report says, "I'm too busy to teach anyone else how to do this," it's time to be concerned.

Your best employees will also resent working with incompetent peers. They see resources being spent on incompetent employees and, again, their morale will suffer.

All too often, an incompetent employee is demoted to a lower-level position in which his contribution to the organization's success is low, but without a reduction in title level or compensation. The decision to reassign, rather than let the employee go, usually involves emotional or legal reasons.

When you play the "demotion game," you usually wind up with the worse problem of having to fire an underperforming employee. If you recognize an employee is a bad fit, move towards letting that employee go—to the extent permitted by laws in your area.

DON'T LIKE WORKING FOR BOSS

Sometimes one of your best people becomes frustrated working for his or her boss and sees no relief from that frustration on the horizon. For example, after an accounting department's star employee gave notice to the manager that he was quitting, a VP of the organization sat down with the accountant to try and change his mind. The accountant explained that he had found a new position because he was frustrated working for his Accounting Manager. The manager (a nice and personable man) was nonetheless disorganized and often changed his mind about assignments after his subordinates had put a lot of effort into those assignments. The accountant added he would not be looking to leave if someone had recognized the situation and done something about it.

The VP had known for some time that the Accounting Manager was a good accountant, but not up to the duties of being a manager. The VP decided he wanted to keep the staff accountant (because he had greater potential to make future contributions to the organization) and that the Accounting Manager should relinquish his position. The VP persuaded the Accounting Manager to resign by offering a good severance package and to pay for the services of an outplacement firm to help him find new employment. As soon as this was accomplished, he started recruiting someone with proven management capabilities to run the accounting department.

DON'T LIKE DOING SOME JOB RESPONSIBILITIES

One reason your best employees may have for giving notice is because they don't like some of their responsibilities. If you want to keep them, look at restructuring their positions. Consider ways to restructure their responsibilities so they no longer do the work they don't like and gain responsibilities in areas of more importance to your organization.

One sales manager who gave notice explained he hated doing administrative tasks. The solution turned out to be giving him an assistant to perform these tasks. As a result, the sales manager changed his mind about leaving. The assistant made the sales manager more efficient by keeping his calendar and aggressively reminding him of time commitments, such as meetings and follow-up phone calls. Yes, there was a cost to this, but the results were worth it.

EMPLOYEE LOOKING FOR A JOB BUT HAS NOT YET GIVEN NOTICE

You may learn that an employee is actively searching for another job, though he has not informed you that he is looking. Don't take the news personally. In the absence of a contract, your employees are free to offer their services anytime, to whomever they wish, at any price.

Let the employee know you are aware of his job search. It is important to handle this conversation calmly and free of emotion. Remember, it is easiest to prevent good people from leaving *before* they decide to leave.

MINIMUM NOTICE TIME OF RESIGNATION

The more time you have to address the situation of a resigning employee, the easier it will be to change his or her mind (or plan the transition when the employee leaves). One way to increase your chances of employees choosing to give adequate notice is to have a policy (if legal in your area) that you will not give references to those who leave without giving appropriate notification.

CONCLUSION

Find out what current and former employees think about working for your organization. Survey them to find out what

> **Look at Glassdoor and similar websites for comments from employees about your work environment.**

they think about working for your organization. If the results indicate some employees have negative feelings about their jobs, you have a chance to do something about it.

Also, research websites where you can see reviews from current and former employees. Determine whether the complaints are valid and, if so, what you can do about them. Negative comments from former, disgruntled employees often skew these sites towards negative reviews. Even companies universally considered "great" find it hard to get perfect ratings.

> **Conducting exit interviews may be the key to making changes that keep good employees.**

Conduct exit interviews with departing employees. Identify things that need correction, so others do not leave. Taking actions to correct any problems will lead to your employees enjoying work more and likely staying with your organization.

In one exit interview, an employee shared her frustration at working for a manager who did not follow through and often changed his mind about things he asked her to do. Informed of this, the manager focused on correcting these patterns and his leadership improved dramatically. Employees in this improved work environment enjoyed work more and were more motivated.

CONCLUSION

After reading my book, your challenge is to avoid falling back into habits that keep you from becoming a High-Impact Manager. You now have the tools to do things differently, so make the habits of High-Impact Managers become part of your DNA. Use what you've learned in this book as your roadmap to a new way of managing that brings about a higher level of impact for your organization. Implement the habits of High-Impact Managers in the same way you would view achieving any other goal. Identify what you need to change about how you currently do things. Create a plan with strategies, deadlines and benchmarks for making it happen.

I promise, when you *stop* the habits holding you back and *start* implementing the tools in this book, you will become a High-Impact Manager.

Good luck!
Allen E. Fishman

CPSIA information can be obtained
at www.ICGtesting.com
Printed in the USA
FFOW02n0101031117
41832FF

9 780996 667210